LOVED AND PROTECTED

BROKEN PIECES RESTORED!

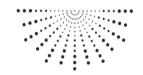

DONNA WEISSER

MIRAMARE
PONTE

Book Production by Miramare Ponte Press

Cover design by Danijela Mijailovic

Paperback ISBN-13: 978-1-7374862-0-6

eBook ISBN-13: 978-1-7374862-1-3

Library of Congress Control Number: 20219133

CONTENTS

ACKNOWLEDGMENTS

I would like to extend a special thanks to my good friends, Linda Smith and Marcy Pusey, for the many hours they invested in editing and formatting this book to bring it to life. Thank you also to the many friends who have encouraged me to write a book and share these many miracles God does for everyday people like me.

This book is dedicated to all of you who may be struggling to believe God will **Love and Protect** *you. As I relate the many incidents in my life, it is my hope that faith will arise in your heart to believe God for your breakthroughs.*

BLIND FAITH

Many people are born with a silver spoon in their mouths, so to speak, due to family position and wealth. I too was born of privilege, but not of financial wealth. My parents, grandparents, and my great-grandparents were all ministers, three generations who provided me a truly rich heritage in the knowledge of Jesus Christ. When God called my parents to go minister to Native American people, they immediately obeyed. Like Abraham, they left family and friends behind in California and headed east with my brother Richard, age five, and me, age twelve, not even knowing where God would lead us. We traveled through Arizona and God nudged us on. When we reached the area of Grants, New Mexico, the Lord spoke to Mama's heart: "This is where I need you." After a few inquiries, they discovered a Navajo reservation was not far from town and that a couple had established a mission in town.

The missionaries invited our family to join in the ministry with them as their assistants. Dad accepted the responsibility of driving the bus through the reservation to pick up the Native Americans for service. My brother and I so enjoyed tagging along for the long drive. The ruts in the road were so deep, Dad could practically let go of the wheel and allow the bus to drive itself. All the way to church the people sang praises to God, so by the time we arrived we were already an hour into worship. After church we stopped at a grocer in town and everyone bought snacks of soda, chips, and candy. It was such a treat for them since there were no stores on the reservation. Then the bus once again followed the ruts, winding its way from hogan to hogan, dropping off our passengers as they continued to sing in Navajo and English. They really loved to worship! One of their favorite songs was "Take This Whole World but Give Me Jesus."

One special day we were invited into a hogan. The wife was making "Paper Bread" on an open fire in the middle of her hogan. Her toddler kept trying to touch the fire and we were frightened for him. As we pushed him away, his mother said, "Him touch it once, him no touch it again." Seated on the dirt floor beside the fire, she dipped her calloused hand into a runny blue cornmeal batter, then ran it ever so quickly across the searing hot grill. Immediately, she peeled the blue paper-thin bread off the surface and placed it on top of the stack she had created on the dirt floor. When she was ready to serve, she simply threw away the bottom piece. I didn't care much for the Paper Bread as it lacked flavor and texture. Another woman was making Navajo Indian Bread in an oven outdoors. That bread is like a delicious thick tortilla. They eat it plain, just fresh out of the oven, but how I would have loved to drench it in butter!

The drums began to beat and the men began to dance. They wore beautiful headdresses of elaborately colored feathers, bare chests adorned with breastplates of beads, with anklets of brilliantly colored feathers. They danced for hours, whirling and twirling with such energy as their feet kept step to every beat of the drums.

After a couple of years, my parents once again felt it was time to move on. Just as before, we headed east not knowing for sure where we were to go. As our tired little car finally climbed the hill approaching Albuquerque, New Mexico, they knew in their spirits that we were in our new hometown.

It was in junior high school in Albuquerque that I met Miriam Owens and we began a life-long friendship. Miriam was a cute brunette with naturally curly hair. She wore it in a short bobbed hairdo to make the curls more manageable. We were physically quite opposites: Miriam about 5'1" and I, 5'6"; she with her short brown hair and I with long blonde hair; she was well endowed and I, well, let's just say that I was a late bloomer. We shared everything together, including our high school infatuation for a boy named Bill. Miriam and I were only freshmen and Bill was a senior, but that didn't stop us from fantasizing that one of us would win his heart.

One night after church, Miriam and I went out to Dad's car to talk while we waited for my parents. We were not aware that my little brother Richard was already in the backseat hiding on the floorboard. We began to share our deepest thoughts when, much to our embarrassment, up he popped. "I'm gonna go tell Bill," he taunted. Quick as a flash, out the door of the car and into the church he ran with the speed of an Olympic racer.

In the car, we were dying of humiliation. We heard Richard holler loud enough for the entire congregation to hear, "My sister and Miriam want to know what it would be like to kiss you!"

Bill, being the confident young man that he was, quickly made his way out to the car and teasingly asked, "So, I hear two girls want to know what it would be like to kiss me. Who wants to go first?" With cheeks on fire we slid down into the seat and died. A couple of years later, Bill married Jan, a pretty, sophisticated college girl, and all our dreams of Bill were shattered.

We attended the Foursquare Church in Albuquerque, under the leadership of Pastor Phil and Sharon Hyde. Pastor Hyde was also the local Presbyter, and a year after we began attending his church, Pastor Hyde challenged my dad to pioneer a second Foursquare Church on the west side of town. Accepting the challenge, our family moved to a new tract of homes in a mountain area called Snow Vista and began the new church in our 3-bedroom home. On Saturdays we went house to house inviting our neighbors to attend church. On Sundays we woke up early to place folding chairs in every room of the house for Sunday school classes in the bedrooms and the church service in the living room. It was not comfortable but we dealt with it and God began to send in one family after another.

Dad worked very hard as a cement truck driver to support our family and then as a pastor on the weekends. But he didn't mind because of his deep love for the Lord and zeal to bring others to Christ. When Dad's secular job ended and there was no money to pay the rent on the house, which was also our budding church, Mother contacted the rental office to explain the delay and promised to pay as soon as possible. The bookkeeper's ledger showed that month's rent was already paid! God's miraculous provision!

The congregation soon outgrew our living room and a church building was secured. It was in that church, at the age of sixteen, that I began teaching others God's Word. It was my privilege to teach the two- and three-year-olds. There was one little guy I will always remember. Bobby was only two years old and was forever under the table. When I questioned him as to why he was under the table his response was, "looking for bugs." He was adorable with his jet black hair and his chubby little rosy cheeks.

When I served the children snacks I used the opportunity to teach them to pray over their food. One day, as Bobby's mother placed the food on their table, Bobby's dad began to eat without asking a blessing. Bobby, then three years old, boldly instructed his dad, "Gotta pray."

His dad, who was not a religious man, answered, "I don't gotta pray."

As he began again to take a bite, little Bobby said in a firmer command, "Gotta pray!" Again, his father ignored the little fellow and tried to get on with the meal. This time little Bobby, with hands on his hips and the firmest voice a three-year-old could muster, declared, "YOU GOTTA PRAY!"

His mother told me it was all she could do to keep from laughing out loud as this dad, now humble, began to stumble through a blessing. My heart was full of joy to know my teaching was making a difference in this little one and perhaps touching his father's heart, also.

2

THE WAY PROVIDED

G od began to give me the desire to attend Bible college. Miriam also felt the call of God to enroll. My parents were very supportive of my decision but Miriam's were not, as they were not church attenders and thought Bible college was a waste of time and money. In June of 1967, after graduation from high school, I felt I was to go to L.I.F.E. (Lighthouse of Foursquare Evangelism) Bible College in Los Angles, California. I applied and the college suggested perhaps I should wait one year until I had more finances. I knew I belonged there so I responded with what I knew:

My God shall supply all my needs according to his riches in glory by
Christ Jesus.
   —Philippians 4:19

The dean agreed and I was admitted. Now, how was I to get there? Miriam was also accepted and she too needed miracles of finances—I, because my parents could not afford tuition, and Miriam because her parents were unwilling for her to enroll.

My dad's mother, Fern Wede, owned a trailer park in the Los Angeles area. She called and asked Dad if he could possibly drive out to California to help her with a problem. Grandma went on to say that if he would come out in August, she would pay for his gas. There was our answer! We could ride with Dad free of cost, have his protection and guidance to get jobs when we arrived, and his help getting settled in! To arrive in August was fine with the college dorms and gave us a month to work and save for needed expenses.

My parents were willing to allow me to go, even though it meant seeing me move to California. Miriam's parents were not so keen on the idea, as Miriam was the baby of the family and it would mean an empty nest. Nevertheless, on the day we left they gave her their blessing. We both knew God was calling us.

An insurance company hired me the first day we sought employment and Miriam found work the very next day. God provided finances.

My job was on the 19th floor of the building. One day, I went to work not feeling very well. As the day progressed I suddenly felt very ill. The room began to sway before me. Was I coming down with the flu? My thought was, *How will I ever get back to the dorm on the city transit?* Then I heard someone yell out, "Earthquake!" My silly first thought was relief that I wasn't terribly ill after all. Thankfully, although our sky-high building swayed back and forth drastically, we were not injured. Thank You, God.

I was assigned two roommates in the dorm: Miriam and Terry. The first couple of weeks we didn't get along at all. Terry was a carefree, free-spirited individual and in true character, would drop her clothes, books, and personal items everywhere. I was a neat freak and found it difficult to function in that chaos. The friction became so tense we went to the dorm mom and asked to be reassigned. Mom Morgan used great wisdom when she made us a deal. Her instruction was for us to pray together every night for a week, and then if we still wanted to move, she would take care of it. We respected her wisdom, and by the end of the week, we loved one another like sisters. This was such a valuable lesson for us to learn how to handle conflict in future life situations.

Terry began to date a young man named Steve. Steve worked as a parking lot attendant on the rooftop of the building across the street from our dorm room. Our dorm room was on the same level as his parking lot. Whenever he wanted to say hello to Terry, he would whistle and Terry would run to the window and throw open the curtains without first checking to see if we were all dressed. We quickly learned to hit the deck when we heard his whistle and it soon became a standing joke.

Although college days were extremely demanding with hardly a moment to breathe, they were also some of the best days of my life. The dorm had a piano room for us to practice our lessons, far enough from the bedrooms so we did not disturb others. Since I worked full-time and went to night classes, the only time I could get in my required hour of practice was about 6 a.m. Then there was breakfast, city transit to work and home again, followed by dinner, the four hours of night school five nights a week, homework, and eventually bed for a few much needed hours of sleep. Weekends were still busy with laundry, additional homework, church attendance, and required hours of volunteer ministry, and to our delight—dates!

I was dating both Wesley and David. I met David when he came to our Albuquerque church as an evangelist. Whenever he came to the L.A. area he stopped by the dorm and we squeezed in a date. At Christmas time we had a date lined up, so in an effort to look my best for him, I bought a new dress, donned my new coat, and worked an hour on my hair. The only comment he made was, "I don't care for your hair being up. It makes you taller than me." I was crushed. Men!

I met Wesley when I purchased my textbooks at the college bookstore where he worked as the cashier. Wesley was older than I by nine years. He had already completed four years in the Navy and graduated L.I.F.E. the year before I arrived at school. We began to date almost immediately.

I had no idea that random meeting in the bookstore would change my life.

FINGER-LICKING GOOD

I wanted to make a chicken dinner for Wesley for his birthday. A friend said I could use her apartment kitchen, so immediately after work I rushed to the local grocery store. I prepared beautifully browned fried chicken, fruit salad, and rice. We sat down to eat. Were we in for a surprise with our first bite of chicken! In my haste, I had bought a stewing chicken. I can still visualize our heads vibrating up and down like cartoon characters as our teeth attempted to sink into that tough bird. After feeding our party of six we still had an entire chicken left. It is a good thing I prepared an abundance of fruit salad and rice. We all had a good laugh.

Halfway through my school year, Wesley accepted a position as pastor of the Fortuna Foursquare Church on the beautiful coastal area of northern California. The position included a charming new three-bedroom parsonage with open beam ceilings, located behind the church on about a half acre of land. Wesley arrived at the house with only his car and his suitcase in hand. He wrote that the house, bare of furnishings, made him feel very lonely. As time progressed, he was able to buy furnishings and make it his home.

We continued to correspond and Wesley asked me to marry him. I felt definitely called to the ministry and I knew I loved him, but I wanted to be sure of God's will for my life. I spent a sleepless night in prayer before giving Wesley my "YES!"

The first year of college whizzed by in the blink of an eye, and by the end of the year, Miriam and I both found ourselves engaged to men called to be pastors. On June 21, 1969, Miriam was married. I was her Maid of Honor. They honeymooned and then returned by the next weekend to enable Miriam to be my Matron of Honor.

My parents resigned the church in Albuquerque and moved to the L.A. area to help my elderly grandmother by managing her mobile home park for her. Since their move and my wedding were during the same month, my dad's sister, Gloria, volunteered to help me with my wedding. We chose to hold the wedding in the Panorama City Foursquare Church where I served my required ministry hours during my freshman year of Bible college. Aunt Gloria adorned the sanctuary and reception hall with many beautiful wedding props from her church. The foyer was decked with gorgeous floral arrangements and sculptured trees, the reception hall draped in soft pink netting and floral pieces. My bridesmaids wore delicate pink chiffon dresses and carried carnations. Everything was lovely and ready. Or was it?

THE SNEAKY HAND

As the wedding began, Aunt Gloria suddenly remembered a very important detail she had overlooked—our communion glass and plate were empty! I noticed the empty vessels as I stood in front of the minister at the beginning of the ceremony and wondered how he would handle the situation. Then, to our amusement, Wesley and I saw a hand reaching between the panels of drapes behind the minister. The hand felt along the table until it found the empty glass and then disappeared behind the drapes, only to reappear again with the now full glass. Then, now groping the table for the empty plate, the hand once again disappeared behind the drapes and returned the plate with the required bread. It was all we could do to keep from laughing out loud. The poor pastor began to turn red as he was sure he must have said something wrong. The traditional full skirt of my satin bridal gown prevented anyone else from seeing the hand. I have laughed many times since as I have shared this cherished wedding memory.

After we were married, we immediately traveled to Fortuna to enable Wesley to continue pastoring there. I was so frightened, wondering if the people would accept me since I was only nineteen years old. My fears turned out to be unfounded. I was not only accepted as their pastor's new wife, but I was loved and encouraged. Miriam and her husband Mel went to Booneville, Missouri, where they too began to pastor. They continued there for 42 years until my beloved friend passed away in 2015. Mel has continued to faithfully pastor there.

On the way down to our wedding, Wesley had car trouble that took up all the cash he had planned to use for a mini honeymoon. So, being totally broke, we ate dry bologna sandwiches as we drove to our new home. Fortuna is near the Oregon border. It was a long, hard drive of 626 miles. When we finally arrived at our new home, we found many cards in the mail with checks in them, but due to the lateness of the hour, we couldn't cash any of them. Expecting to honeymoon for a couple of days, Wesley had emptied his refrigerator before leaving for our wedding. So despite a pocket full of checks, we were still without a good meal. Scouting the cupboards produced some pancake batter and syrup so that became our first meal in our new home.

PASTOR'S WIFE AT NINETEEN

During the week before my first service in the new church, Wesley coerced me into practicing a duet with him to sing on Sunday morning. On Sunday, just after introducing me as his wife, he announced, "and she is going to sing for you." He then went and sat down. I was more terrified to make a scene than to sing so I made it through my first solo.

Wesley knew I was terribly shy, so to break me out of my shell, a couple of weeks later he volunteered me to be the guest soloist for a well-attended ladies community luncheon. They printed the announcement in the local newspaper, and then he presented me with a copy. God used Wesley's antics to launch me into ministry. From that day forward I continued to gain confidence and expanded ministries as Wesley gently urged me to teach classes and lead Bible study groups while God placed His hand of anointing upon me.

Fortuna was a small logging and fishing community. Things went well there until the men of the city went on strike. There was absolutely no work in the area and so no monies came in to support the church. Wesley continued to sell Fuller Brush as a supplement to our salary, but when the full impact of the strike hit, people stopped buying his wares and there was no salary available from the church.

We lived from day to day, returning pop bottles we found and scraping up change to get more vegetables to add to our soup pot. When things just didn't change week after week, *fear* totally gripped my young heart. One day I went to the refrigerator and found only one carrot and one tomato. I threw myself across the bed sobbing, "We're gonna starve." This was the first of many lessons in *walking by faith*.

We didn't starve. Wesley called his supervisor who recommended that we move to Red Bluff. The supervisor asked a retired school teacher in the area to hold services in Fortuna since she would not be reliant on the church for income.

In January, I became pregnant with our darling daughter, Cheri, who was born the following September, not too long after our move to Red Bluff.

DANGER AHEAD

With our station wagon and U-haul trailer fully loaded, we began our journey to Red Bluff, California. As we drove along it began to rain. Suddenly, the trailer tire hit some loose gravel and the vehicle began to slide. The trailer slid off the road, dragging our car helplessly along. When the car came to a stop, my door was leaning against a telephone pole and the trailer was dangling down the embankment. We sat still and prayed, afraid to move for fear our trailer would drag us down the mountain slope after it. Within minutes of our prayer, God sent a Caltrans vehicle along to rescue us. The mighty vehicle gently pulled us to safety and we were once again on our way.

On our first Sunday in the church several people gave their hearts to God. These people coming to know Jesus as their Savior made the difficult trip worth it all.

When we left Fortuna that morning, it was a cool 60 degrees as Fortuna is a beautiful coastal city. But that afternoon when we arrived in Red Bluff the temperature was over 100 degrees with high humidity due to the Sacramento River that runs through the area. The extreme temperature change was not an easy adjustment for anyone, but I found it even more challenging as I was now five months pregnant. One day late in my pregnancy, I was feeling particularly uncomfortable with the 110 degree heat and humidity. As I sat in the doctor's office awaiting my regular pregnancy visit, I began to feel sorry for myself until I saw another patient sitting across from me. This poor girl was wearing a full body cast and was suffering with a broken back *and* was great with child. In an effort to carry her baby to full term, she was confined to bedrest except for her visits to the doctor to have the cast shaved to allow the baby more growing room. I suddenly didn't feel so sorry for myself.

There were still more lessons to be learned about *living by faith* as this church was struggling financially as well. They provided us with a little one-bedroom shack of a house and gave us $25 a week in salary if it was available after the church bills were paid. The shack had been built as a *temporary* home years before we arrived. It had no foundation. The kitchen floor had a high point in the middle with a quarter-inch gap between the floors and the walls. We used to joke saying, "If a glass of water were poured in the middle of the floor, it wouldn't know which way to roll." One of the closets consisted only of the framework and tar paper but no sheetrock or exterior wall. One day a friend tripped while entering the closet and fell through the tar paper wall, landing outside the house! We laughed so hard at the look on her face as she looked up at us from outside the home.

Shortly after we moved into this parsonage, the swamp cooler quit functioning and there was no money to fix it. Since a lot of my slacks were heavy material due to Fortuna's cooler climate, I stripped down to only a maternity smock and panties in an effort to survive the heat. Then later that day, without any notice of their arrival, I heard my husband entering the house talking to several men from our church board. With not a moment to flee for cover in our shotgun-style house, I did the only thing I could do: I quickly sat down and pulled the smock over my knees and there I sat as a prisoner. My husband had no clue of my dilemma, so there I sat as the men went from room to room noting needed repairs. After the men left and I recovered from my embarrassment, we had a good laugh.

It was while serving in Red Bluff that God blessed us with our first bundle of joy, Cheri Lynn, a beautiful baby girl with lots of dark hair at birth that quickly turned to blonde curls.

SPAGHETTI FOR TWELVE?

With money tight, one Sunday I prepared spaghetti for lunch expecting to feed my family of three and a widow friend with her two sons. As we sat down to eat, another person dropped by and then another and then another. Each time I went back to the pot of spaghetti to serve yet another plate, there was plenty of noodles and plenty of sauce. I firmly believe we received a miracle of God's multiplication that day, very much like the biblical account of the widow's flour and oil that never ran out.

During the time we were in Red Bluff, my parents asked if my brother Richard could come live with us. They were weary battling his drug addiction. When Rich was only in elementary school, someone got him started on drugs and it continued to be a problem over the years to come. I was only seven years older than Richard so my parents thought perhaps my husband and I could reach him better than they could as older parents.

One night while he was with us, we held him down as he screamed in agony while going through withdrawals. Richard then lived with us drug-free during his junior high years and seemed to be happy.

While attending junior high, Richard was sent to the principal's office. I received a call to come pick up my brother who was suspended. The crime? He had accepted a bet that he would eat a tadpole from the creek that ran just behind the school.

Another day we received a call from the Sacramento police department. Richard had become homesick and decided to cut school and hitchhike home to L.A to see Mom and Dad. He had not asked to go because it would have required missing some school and he thought we would not permit him to make the trip. Just as we arrived in the Sacramento area, our car broke down. Wesley called the local church for help and one of their members, a mechanic, came to our rescue. The mechanic and his wife were such a godly example of Christian love. They housed and fed my brother and us for three days while her husband worked on our jalopy. We had only packed a diaper bag for Cheri as we headed off on our three-hour day trip to rescue Richard. They loaned us their daughter's crib and even her clothes during our stay, which meant sending their children to Grandma's house.

I wish I could say Richard broke completely free of drugs but, unfortunately, he dealt with them the rest of his short life. After graduation from junior high, Richard returned to live with my parents.

God blessed and performed miracles during our ministry in that church. One lady had a tumor the size of a third breast. I laid my hand on it and Wesley placed his hand over mine. As we prayed, I felt the tumor shrink beneath my hand. How marvelous to experience God's mighty power.

WHEREVER GOD LEADS!

One of my husband's former Bible college friends, Frank Stronach, called and asked us if we would like to come and hold a two-week revival in his church in Pasco, Washington. God blessed during the revival and after much prayer, we decided to stay and assist in this pioneer church. Wesley found work as an assisting mortician to support us. Things were going very well and the church grew. So did our little family; our lovely second daughter, Michele, was born. Michele had a sunny disposition from birth and always had a smile. Her daddy nicknamed her "Smiley."

We lived only a block away from Pastor Frank, Rena his wife, and their three children. Our daughters enjoyed playing together with their dollies. One day, their daughter, Mindy, showed Cheri her new "imported" dolly. Not to be outdone, three-year-old Cheri responded, "I have an *important* dolly too."

Life was good in beautiful Washington. We had it all: the ministry was thriving, nice home, friends, steady income, good climate, and now a second beautiful daughter.

Then God asked for the supreme act of faith. Just as he had asked my parents to leave everything and follow Him so many years before, we now felt God calling Wesley to quit his job and go on the evangelistic field. The faith my parents had exhibited when I was twelve blessed me with the ability to step out in faith and follow God's bidding now.

We held a big yard sale and sold everything that would not fit into our car. The neighbors asked where we were headed and when we replied, "Wherever God leads," they told us we were crazy. With the car packed, off we went with Cheri who was now three years old and our newborn, Michele. When we left Washington we only had one service booked. God was faithful to give us one meeting after another for the next year, and our income was equal to his former salary as an apprentice mortician! When we step out of the boat and onto the water, God doesn't let us drown.

One night after a revival ended, the pastor handed us a check but did not invite us out to eat. Checking our funds, we discovered that we had only enough cash to buy Cheri a hamburger at a local fast food stand. As Wesley reached into his pocket to pay, out came more change than before. There was enough money for all of us to have a sandwich! As he approached the pickup window for the burgers, the restaurant owner asked him if we would like to have some fresh french fries that she cooked anticipating more of a crowd than what manifested. Free fries and a burger! God always takes care of his children.

TUMBLEWEEDS AND SAGEBRUSH

O ne of the revival services we booked was in Ridgecrest, California. The pastor there was also the supervisor of all the churches in his division. He asked us to consider pastoring a small church in Johannesburg, California, locally known as Jo'burg. Johannesburg is an isolated desert mountain town of 100 people sandwiched between two other little towns of 100 people out in the middle of the Mojave desert. The nearest grocery store was twenty-five miles away in Ridgecrest. Most of the population was senior retirees which did not appeal to me at all, as I was only twenty-five at the time. When we drove by and looked at the church, everything within me cried, "NOOOOOO!" There was no grass, no flowers, nothing like lushly green Washington.

To make matters worse, the pastor had a car junkyard along the side of the parsonage and car parts scattered across the front yard! The nearest neighbor was two blocks away with only sagebrush and desert sand between houses. There was a mini-mart and gas station in town that still had one of those rubber hoses for the cars to run over to create a dinging noise to alert the attendant that he had a customer.

Jo'burg was so quiet that you could hear the "ding" all over town. With not much else to do, everyone looked out their windows to see who was buying gas. The town had a motto: "If you haven't heard a rumor by noon, start one." There was no way this girl wanted to move to such a desolate town. I prayed and I cried, then I prayed and I cried some more: "Lord, please not there." Then I died to the flesh and said, "Lord, not my will but Yours."

After we had lived in Jo'burg for a short while, I was very depressed and lonely for a friend. God knew my need. A woman about forty-five years old with a small child Michele's age bought the cottage across the street as her weekend getaway home. This little boy, Dean, was years younger than his sisters. Myrna drove up almost every weekend all the way from San Bernardino and became a dear friend. It amazes me how the God of the entire universe loves us so much that He even cared about my need for a friend.

It was in Jo'burg that our darling Debbie was conceived and born in the neighboring city of Ridgecrest. After church on Sunday, Wesley drove the girls to pick Debbie and me up from the hospital. In their excitement to meet their new sister, one of the girls failed to close the car door. As we exited the hospital Wesley asked, "Who left the car door open?" The reply came back, "Debbie did it!" Welcome to the family, baby.

Debbie was born with lots of beautiful thick brown hair that was to remain brown while her two sisters, Cheri and Michele, were fair-haired blondes.

Once we cleared the yard of the former pastor's junk, I began to like Johannesburg. God began to show me the beauty of this new land as I discovered the opalescent wings of the dragonflies and the spring flowers that would carpet the landscape for miles in bursts of glorious yellow and bright purple. It was also interesting in the spring to watch hundreds of tarantulas march down the street in groups of 100 like little armies.

The wind would blow with gusts of up to 100 miles an hour in this mountainous community. Unaware, I opened both the front and back doors of our home and a gust of wind whipped through our house, lifting pictures off the wall and dropping them to the floor like mere pieces of paper in its path. Another day, one such gust blew my little girl off balance and sent her rolling down the hill like a little tumbleweed.

One warm summer night I decided to go for a bike ride. I hopped on my bike while wearing shorts, a tank top, and sandals. As I rounded the corner to begin a downhill section of my excursion, to my dismay, I discovered I could not squeeze my hand brakes. Our sixteen year old foster son had thought he was doing me a favor by tightening up my bike, including my hand grips for the brakes! Instead of being brave and immediately laying the bike over on its side, I continued the steep downhill grade going faster and faster as the bike traveled the four blocks toward Highway 395!

As I crossed into the path of 395, my front tire hit gravel and tossed me like a rag doll into the line of Sunday night traffic headed south. God was with me. A car pulling a trailer behind it was able to stop within a foot of me with no injury to its driver or the vehicles behind it. I, however, did have massive road burns, especially to my face and shoulders which hit the pavement first before scraping my knees and toes. When assisted to the side of the road, all I could say was, "My big toe hurts." My unprotected toe, due to the sandals, had a torn toenail and was throbbing. I really didn't feel any pain in my raw, almost entirely bloody face or my shoulder caps with their huge bloody scrapes. Miraculously, I had no broken bones. I was grateful that Mom and Dad had decided to come for a visit and they arrived just a few minutes after my accident. Mom was such a blessing to me as she assisted in the housework and especially the lifting of the baby in and out of her crib, a task I could not accomplish due to the massive scabs on my shoulders extending to my upper arms.

The only schoolhouse in town operated like a one-room schoolhouse. The teacher and one teacher's aide taught lessons to all the twenty-eight children from Kindergarten through 6th grade. These children also received additional one-on-one attention from those of us who volunteered to assist. Cheri was the only first grader, which proved to be an advantage. As she daily listened to the older children recite their lessons, she advanced very rapidly and gained excellent reading skills.

One day, we went into Ridgecrest to buy groceries. I gathered my groceries and went to the cashier to pay. To my dismay, my grocery money was gone. I raced through the store but it was not to be found. Returning to the car, I just knew Wesley would be so upset with me for losing all our money. However, he just sweetly said for me not to worry about it, God would take care of us. I cried all the way back to Johannesburg.

When we pulled into the driveway, I couldn't believe my eyes. There on the front porch were five large paper bags full of groceries! Who? Where could they have come from? We only had a 7-11 type convenience store in Jo'burg. Whoever brought us these groceries either brought them to us off their own shelves or came ahead of us from Ridgecrest. God had supplied our need in a marvelous way. We never did learn our benefactor's name but praised God for his willingness to obey God's prompting to meet our need.

One day Myrna called me to request that Michele be the flower girl in her daughter Melanie's wedding and Dean would be the ring bearer. I inquired about the dress and Myrna told me to just buy a light yellow Easter dress. The bridesmaids were going to wear colonial type floor-length dresses in lemon yellow and carry parasols; the groomsmen were wearing white tuxedos with top hats and walking sticks. I searched everywhere for what I thought would be an appropriate dress and found nothing to my liking. All the Easter dresses were short-skirted and modern. I prayed and asked God to help me pick out a pattern and yardage. I chose a lemon yellow chiffon with mutton sleeves and a peplum with a floor-length skirt. When we arrived at the wedding, Myrna was as amazed as I was: not only was Michele's dress chiffon like the bridesmaids' dresses but it was the exact shade of yellow as theirs! The Holy Spirit had directed me perfectly in my choices. The Bible says in the book of James, "If any man lack wisdom, let him ask God who gives to all men liberally." He doesn't mind being invited into our daily lives to help with our trivial needs. Trouble is, sometimes we just don't ask Him.

Grandma had sold her trailer court and moved near her daughter, Margie, to retire. Mom and Dad began to sense God calling then to leave the Los Angeles area and come to our area to pastor. For several weekends they drove up to our area and checked out towns within a twenty-five to fifty mile radius of our home. They knew God wanted them in that area but they didn't know exactly where at that time.

I decided to repaint my kitchen and I found myself thinking, "What color would Mom like?" I puzzled over the thought and God spoke to my heart that we would soon be leaving and Mom and Dad would indeed be the new pastors there. Mom and Dad loved Johannesburg and stayed for the next seven years.

9

WHAT? FORGIVE THEM?

S anger presented us with many new challenges. The congregation in Sanger was split into three factions before we arrived. The problem we inherited was that the former pastor's daughter got pregnant out of wedlock and the people, lacking love, couldn't cope with the situation. One group said to forgive her and restore her to her ministries while she was still pregnant, since she had repented and even asked the congregation for forgiveness. The second faction demanded if she was really repentant she should have an abortion! Can you believe that? The third group took the position that if she would give the baby away and her boyfriend would leave the church then she could minister again in their church. What a mess! Wesley asked the congregation to come together in prayer about the disunity. Each group would come separately but refused to come together for a united prayer.

In Sanger, Wesley once again worked as an apprentice mortician to supplement a seriously inadequate church salary. It was convenient since our church was on one side of the parsonage and the mortuary was on the other.

MY DIAMOND IS MISSING

As I was in and out of the car shopping from store to store one day, I glanced at my hand and notice my quarter-carat diamond was missing from my wedding ring. I felt sick. I asked God, "If my stone is anywhere that would allow me to find it, please help me retrieve it, Lord." I went about my day and when I returned home I began to vacuum my shag carpets. Just as I was about to move the vacuum head forward, something sparkled in the sunlight. There, nestled deep into the long shag fibers, was my diamond. "God, You are so good to me," I sobbed in delight.

DOUBLE YOUR FAMILY

Another day, a neighbor lady came frantically to my door. Donna Mary asked me if I could please watch her three children while she went to be with her husband who had just been in a terrible motorcycle accident. Of course, I was glad to help. Later the same evening, the police came to my door with some terrible news: Donna Mary's husband had died at the scene of the accident when his motorcycle exploded on impact and horribly burned his body. Donna Mary had viewed the charred body, went into shock, and had to be hospitalized. The officer asked if we would keep the children for the night. A week later the hospital called us to ask if we could continue taking care of the children because Donna Mary was in a complete mental breakdown and was not responding to treatment.

During the following weeks her oldest son Gary, age seven, reverted to bed-wetting; her daughter Sarah, age three, had nightmares; and her baby boy Georgie, age two, just missed Mommy. After several weeks in our care, the authorities notified us the children would soon be placed in three separate foster homes because none of the existing foster homes wanted three children. Not wanting to see the children further traumatized by being separated from one another, we went to court and applied for temporary custody which the judge willingly granted. I wish our congregation had been as understanding and willing as the judge. These people actually railed on us for taking the children in! I have never seen a group of "Christians" with such a lack of love. Adding the three children to our own family of three children gave me six children under the age of seven years. Nevertheless, I managed to have them all at church clean and on time. And I still continued to play the organ for song service and teach a Sunday school class, so I never could understand the basis for any complaint.

Sarah and our Debbie were in preschool together. The school nurse sent them home with the unhappy news that both girls had head lice. I began to treat their hair with medicated shampoo followed by the tedious task of combing their waist-length hair with a tiny nit comb. This was problematic enough but then all the other four children also became infested. I shampooed each child, sprayed furniture and bedding daily, and yet these persistent pests continued to thrive. I would manage to rid one child but with the others still infected with the lice, the others would then reinfect him.

I became so traumatized after two weeks of battling these insects that I had a nightmare that lice were crawling across my ceiling and falling down upon me. In desperation I called the health department for advice. I did not like what I heard. Their advice: carry all six of their mattresses outside every morning and into the sunlight. Daily wash all their bedding and pajamas in the hottest bleach water possible, spray all carpets and furniture *and* re-shampoo all six children's' hair before bed! What a job! Wesley and I followed the exhausting instructions and within days all of the lice were gone, but I still had to comb and comb their hair to remove all the nits before they were allowed back into school.

Things went pretty smooth after that, that is until Christmastime. The children were home on Christmas break when one child began to complain of a sore, swollen neck and had a rash. Another child had a fever, headache, and vomiting. Another had vomiting and the rash. Yet another the swollen neck and rash, etc., etc., etc. Completely bewildered, I gathered all six of my poor babies into the car and off to the doctor's office we went with our mysterious plague. To my dismay, after examining my sickly brood, the doctor returned with the glorious news: "Congratulations, you have measles, mumps and the flu. Merry Christmas!"

Life was also at times humorous as I got to know my new wards. One day, as I drew the bath water for Debbie and Georgie, Debbie slipped out to our driveway and was climbing on the fender of the church bus when she lost her footing and fell head first onto the asphalt driveway. Gary came running into the house: "Donna, Donna, Debbie just fell off the church bus and her head went S P L A T all over the driveway." When the blood returned to my white-as-a-sheet body, I ran to the driveway with visions of Debbie's head cracked wide open and brains pouring out. To my significant relief, Debbie only had a one-inch cut on her forehead that did not even merit stitches. I had just learned that Gary was quite the drama king!

During the year the children lived with us, Gary developed a deep love for God, and it blessed me tremendously when he shared with me that when he grew up he thought he would like to be a pastor. Gary was growing closer to God. I wish I could say the same for our congregation.

During a church membership meeting, complaint after complaint was rained upon us. One ridiculous accusation was that we allowed our children to go barefoot in the parsonage front yard during the summer. Who doesn't let their children play in their yard barefoot during the summer? And, after all, the parsonage was our home. Then there was the ongoing complaint of Donna Mary's children being in our care. And last but not least, they were angry that we would not ask any of the other three factions to leave the church. Our daughter, Cheri, who was now seven, had come into the meeting just long enough to hear a bit of these hateful words. When I went to check on her she was sobbing. "Why don't these people love us, Mommy?"

After a year, Donna Mary finally recovered and took her children home to live with her. Donna Mary received Jesus as her Savior and began to put her life back together.

After Donna Mary's children returned home, I once again gave birth. This fourth child was a son, James William, whom we decided to nickname Billy.

During my pregnancy, I worked at the local JCPenney, which required me to be on my feet all day. When Billy was born, he measured twenty-four inches in length. The doctor could not believe this measurement was accurate so he sent the nurse out to measure Billy again. She returned with "twenty-four inches." Unable still to believe his ears, the doctor measured my son himself and returned saying, "Congratulations, you have a man-child." My husband was delighted. After three lovely daughters, finally a son.

God began speaking to Wesley's heart to preach a very difficult message. Wesley wrestled with God to be sure he was hearing correctly and not in error, so he fasted and prayed. Sunday came and in obedience he preached what God placed in his heart. The entire congregation was angered because they still had not learned how to love or forgive. The following Sunday, no one came to church. Wesley and I sat in the pews and began to pray. God sent in forty-five visitors and we had Church! One of the visitors, without being told what had transpired that morning, spoke words from God confirming to Wesley that he had been obedient and the people were in rebellion to God. This is what the Bible refers to as a Word of Knowledge. We were greatly encouraged.

Although we did not see many positive results in Sanger, we left knowing we had been totally obedient servants as we had preached "love" and modeled "Love your neighbor as yourself" when we took in our neighbor's three little ones.

MIRACLE? TAKE TWO

J ust thirty minutes east of Sanger is a little farming community called Orange Cove, so named for its many orange orchards. We began to commute to the Assembly of God church in Orange Cove and were soon voted in as their new pastors.

Housing was difficult to find in Orange Cove. One house I looked at had metal cupboards, one of which was hanging on the wall only by a prayer, and in the bathroom there was a large hole in the sheetrock. The landlord thought he was going to rent the house as it was. I found a perfect house in the paper and it was near the church. It was a beautiful three-bedroom brick home with a well-manicured yard. There was a problem though: the asking rent was $100 a month over our budget. A week later, I took Wesley by the house just to show him the exterior and a miracle occurred. A woman was standing in the front doorway, and when she saw us, she motioned for us to come. As I approached her, she asked if we were the couple who had come to see the house. I explained to her that we had been interested but the asking price was $100 over budget. She then informed us that the house had been listed with a realtor and now she was managing it herself and had dropped the price by $100 a month! She went on to say that she was there to show the house to a couple who had called, but since they failed to show up, if we wanted the home it was ours! We lived comfortably in that home with our four children and a foster daughter, Diane.

Orange Cove offered very little for children to do, so after prayerfully seeking the Lord, I felt I was to start a little girls' club that would be a blend of something like Scouts but adding biblical teaching.

Our church was located across the street from the elementary school. I approached the principal and asked for permission to hand out flyers after school to announce the new girls' club. He was so excited he offered to print one for every girl and distribute them through the teachers. The first week, fifty little girls showed up and the girls' club was off to a glorious start. Week after week these little girls enthusiastically came and received the Word of God.

After a year, the landlord of the brick house gave us thirty-day notice to move because they had decided to return to Orange Cove to retire. Now we not only needed a house but we had just been asked if we could take in another teen named Sarah.

"Lord, we need another miracle to find a home for a family of eight," I prayed. At the water department I inquired whether they had knowledge of any large homes coming available for rent. The lady at the desk directed me to a farmhouse in the country. I mistakingly thought she meant the gorgeous two-story farm house on Monson Avenue that I had always loved, so I immediately drove to the home to check it out. When I arrived, two college-aged men were frantically moving furniture out as hurriedly as possible. When I told them that the lady from the water department had sent me, they looked horrified.

The guys were skipping out on their rent and had not notified the landlord or anyone else they were moving. The young men reluctantly gave me the landlord's phone number, making me promise not to call him before the following day. Within days we had rented the huge new home God had prepared for us. When I went in to turn the water on in our name, I thanked the lady at the desk for the lead. She laughed and said, "That isn't the address I was sending you to." God had just done another miracle to provide us with just the right housing.

The Munson Street home was huge. It was an old-fashioned two-story home with a formal dining room that had a built-in china cupboard with lead glass inserts and an eat-in kitchen. The dinette area of the kitchen had windows on three sides that let in lots of morning sun and a restful view of the grape vineyards. It was a delightful nook for morning devotions. The ceilings of the home were ten feet high and it had four bedrooms that measured fourteen by twenty feet each. The entire house was enormous and just perfect for a family of eight!

From the upstairs you could see for a mile in every direction, what magnificent views! The children could also see the school bus coming. One would call out to the others, "The bus!" Everyone began to scramble and the house would thunder as six pairs of feet ran down the stairs. As the last child left through the front door, the entire house gave a gentle sigh.

CHERI IS MISSING!

We had family friends stop by for a visit, Ed and Joyce with their daughter Rebecca. Ed was Rebecca's stepdad and was extremely strict. Rebecca had not been allowed to date nor even attend dances or football games while she was in high school. Weary of this lifestyle, she determined to run away in her stepfather's car. After Ed retired for the night, Rebecca slipped the keys from his pocket and stole his cash. Our daughter Cheri was moved with compassion and didn't want to see Rebecca go alone, so she left us a loving note and said she would be back soon. The offering collected from Sunday was in our home waiting to be deposited the next day and, although she knew that it was there, she didn't touch it. Not a dime was taken. Where would the girls go with so little cash? I was worried sick because Rebecca didn't even have a driver's license.

When Ed awoke the next morning he was livid! He didn't take any action the first day but by Sunday morning, three days later, he was threatening that if Rebecca wasn't back with the car by that evening he was going to file charges against both girls for the theft of his car.

My fears were mounting. I was worried to death for the girls' safety, not knowing how well Rebecca could drive, and afraid they could be caught up in human trafficking. And now the thought of criminal charges of *grand theft auto!* I went to the church early that morning and poured out my heart upon the altar. "God, *please* cause my daughter to call me so I can warn her."

Church began and my heart was heavy but then... I heard the church office phone ringing. I left the piano in the middle of a song and ran to answer it. God had answered my prayer; it was Cheri. I was able to warn the girls and they made it home safely before any legal action was taken. God heard this Momma's cry.

TRAGEDY STRIKES

My brother Richard wanted to attend Cheri's junior high graduation but his car was not running properly. I agreed to pick him up and we had a nice visit. However, on the return trip, the conversation became heavy as Richard disclosed that he thought the real reason his wife had not come with him was that she was having an affair. When we arrived at his house, his eyes swelled with tears as he realized the car parked in his driveway belonged to the "other man."

A few weeks later I received a phone call in the middle of the night; it was my brother's wife. Lynn told me that my brother was dead. Richard had been depressed for some time and that day had talked of suicide, even taking a rifle out of the gun cabinet. She said that she called her "friend" to come help her with Richard. When he attempted to wrestle the rifle out of Richard's hand, it went off and the bullet entered Richard's head just above his eyebrow. The Coroner listed the cause of death as "Suspicious," stating that the angle of entry made it almost impossible for Richard to have pulled the trigger himself. The police investigation left the death unsolved due to a lack of evidence in either direction. A week after the funeral, the "friend" moved in with my sister-in-law, so we have always wondered if their story was the whole story and the whole truth.

Lynn called me in the middle of the night and asked me to break the news to my parents. My husband wanted us to go right then, but I decided to wait until morning. I knew it would be difficult enough for them to bear this news while well rested. There was nothing they could do before morning anyway. Telling my parents that their only son, who was just thirty-three years old, was dead was the hardest thing I have ever had to do.

A short while after my brother's death, his two children, Richard Jr., age eight, and Marylynn, only five years old, were placed in foster care and their mother was declared "unfit." I didn't feel physically able to take them in because I had many responsibilities as a pastor's wife, mother of six children, a large home to maintain, and I worked twenty hours a week outside of the home. My parents applied for custody and then began to raise their second family.

STRANGER WITH A KNIFE

To supplement our income, I accepted a part-time job driving the seniors in Orange Cove to eat a hot lunch at our local community center. One day, the boss called and asked if I would temporarily fill in for a larger, eight-hour-a-day route that went from Orange Cove to Fresno twice a day, much like a bus route. The driver who normally drove that route had injured his back and was unable to work. After I drove into Fresno, my break time allotted me twenty minutes in downtown Fresno. I parked the work van and thought I would just walk through the area of the stores and "window shop."

As I walked along, I looked up and saw a man approaching me with a large knife in his hand alongside his leg. I gave him a puzzled look and he responded by raising it menacingly above his shoulder and running toward me. I screamed, "JESUS" and began to run. I ran into a local store and peeked out but I could not see him. Witnesses said they observed the man chasing me, but the police could not find him. I am so thankful that our God is "an ever-present help in the time of trouble."

During our time in Orange Cove I continued to grow in ministry, and God used me more and more. I began to teach Wednesday night Bible study, lead song service and head up Women's Ministry as well as the weekly girls' club. I was so fulfilled. My ministry was in its prime; we had a good income and comfortable housing. I felt extremely joyful and content.

During our time there, however, Wesley developed some grievous sores in his mouth, underarms, and on his genitals. Doctors diagnosed the sores as Lichen Planus. Normally, a patient may have one variety of the sores, but Wesley had all three known varieties. The doctors said it might be due to Agent Orange that he was exposed to during his military service in Vietnam. Over the next ten years, Wesley was verbally affectionate and brought me flowers but stopped all kissing and sexual activity because he said he was afraid of infecting me. Then one Sunday morning, without even discussing it with me or mentioning it ahead of time, Wesley stood in the pulpit and offered his resignation as their pastor. He only offered the explanation of declining health. My heart was broken because that meant I had to leave, too. Under the church by-laws I could not even stay on as a member of the congregation. All of my ministries came to a screeching halt.

DOWNHILL LIVES

Our landlord at the Munson Street home had been congenial the whole time we lived in his home, but now all of a sudden he turned on us. He would come and pound on the door at the break of dawn and yell at me, cursing, saying that our dogs had scattered trash all through his vineyards. I tried to explain that we didn't even own a dog but it was to no avail, so I would dress and go out to clean up the litter. All while I cleaned the mess, he continued to curse at me. After months of this irritating, irrational behavior, I decided that enough was enough. In my frustration I gave him our thirty days' notice that we were going to move.

The two foster girls had returned to their homes and two of our daughters were now being bussed to the neighboring town of Reedley for high school. Our girls were very active in after-school activities and parents were required to provide transportation home at 10:00 p.m. or 11:00 p.m. So, when we considered the inconvenience of the landlord's behavior and the late-night drives taking twenty minutes each way, we decided to move to Reedley. I didn't take a moment to ask God; I just decided to move.

Our landlord had no problem renting the beautiful home we were in, and he let us know we needed to be out promptly on the 30th as the new family would be moving in on the first of the month. I began to look for a new rental in Reedley and *nothing* was available. We had packed and had the necessary deposit monies but had nowhere to go. On the afternoon of the 30th, we still had nowhere to go. I called out to the Lord desperately for forgiveness in being so brash in my decision and for not inquiring of Him if we should move. I asked God for mercy and for His help. At 5:00 p.m. on the night before we needed to be out of the home, God gave us a tiny three-bedroom apartment and we spent all night moving in. I learned a valuable lesson that day: to always seek the Lord before making big decisions. However, when we do make mistakes, He still loves us and is there to pick us up and set us on the right path again. A year later, I learned that the Munson Street landlord had died from cancer and that his irrational behavior was due to heavy drugs for his pain management.

While I covered the Orange Cove to Fresno transit route for work, they covered my short little route with a local woman who was handicapped. It was her very first job and she was so proud to have it. When it was time for me to return to my route, I told the boss to allow her to just keep it and I would find another job. I didn't have the heart to take the route from her when it brought her so much joy.

WHAT DID I GET MYSELF INTO?

My new job was driving a 78-passenger school bus. I will never forget the first training day I sat behind the wheel of that monstrously big vehicle. My knuckles were white and my back was not even relaxed enough to touch the back of the seat. After hours of training, I still drove in fear—it was so big!

Reedley School Bus Transportation offered me a position as a substitute driver so I began my new career in September 1987. I love children which enabled me to handle seventy-eight students with no problem. At first, there weren't enough hours offered, so I supplemented my income by working across the street at McDonald's during the remainder of breakfast and all of lunch. McDonald's liked my work and also gave me eight to ten hours of work on Saturdays and then forty to fifty hours a week during the summers. I worked both jobs together for several years until I finally received a regular route of my own with Kings Canyon Unified School District. Then I only worked McDonald's in the summers. Both of our daughters, Cheri and Michele, worked with me at the same McDonald's part-time after school and on Saturdays.

Michele and I worked drive-thru as a team. I took the orders and drew the drinks while Michele filled the food portion and presented them at the second window. We had a good laugh together one day. As I was taking an order, a high-school-aged young man at the drive-thru speaker started hitting on me with his best pick-up lines. He was very surprised to see a 38-year-old woman instead of the young lady he thought my voice represented.

After driving the bus for several years, I had achieved a pretty good mastery of maneuvering the 40-foot monster. Later, a new officer took over our renewal test. This officer had never driven a school bus and his expectations of us were ridiculous. He asked us to swerve back and forth around cones going both forward and backward, which was fine and part of a normal test. In addition, however, he created his own test. He expected us to back the bus and then stop EXACTLY three feet from a sawhorse! We were not allowed to turn off the bus and get out to see whether we were more than three feet or less than three feet away. Once we turned off the key, we failed the test if we were not spot on!

When it was my day to test, I was so nervous. I prayed and told the Lord if He wanted me to continue as a driver, He was going to have to help me pass that portion of the test because I knew I couldn't do it on my own. I had a perfect test on all the other portions and then it was time for that backing test. As I neared the sawhorse, it disappeared in both my side mirrors and the rear view mirror. I was driving blind. What was this officer thinking? I whispered, "Lord, help me."

Immediately, the sunlight projected a shadow of the sawhorse on the ground so that I was able to see it in my side mirror. I was now able to use the shadow as my reference point and know when to stop. I turned off the key and went out to the officer. He pulled out his tape measure and to my amazement, the rear of my bus was exactly three feet from this tiny barricade! God is so willing to be part of our everyday lives and to help with our slightest call. He is delighted when His children rely on Him in faith.

Meanwhile, Wesley went into the construction business. He was a very skilled craftsman but, unfortunately, lacked the knowledge of profitable bidding. One particular remodel was an entire apartment complex. He worked for months on the project and had underbid so drastically that it became necessary to use my salary checks to purchase more materials to fulfill the contract.

Week after week he labored and even recruited our children to help. And week after week my salary dissolved until our little family was in a desperate financial state. Our electricity was cut off, so the girls went down to the laundry room to use the hot water to wash up in the sink and use the electricity to curl their hair. We also received an eviction notice and we ran out of groceries. I cried out to the Lord for help and mercy. A family from church stopped by to see us and I was embarrassed to be sitting in the dark. They never asked us about the lights; they just returned a short while later with many bags of groceries. The next morning our lights were also restored. We all thanked God for food and lights and for loving people who met our need. "Lord," I asked, "we have food and lights, but what do we do about the eviction notice? Who will rent to us with this awful blemish on our record?"

There was a large two-story house just a mile from work. I took my next paycheck and timidly approached the landlord with the possibility of renting the home. God granted me favor and this Christian man rented me the house immediately without any background checks. When Wesley returned home from his construction job, I was able to share the good news with him that God had just granted us a mini-miracle.

Even amidst the tragedy of losing my brother, ending my job, making decisions without asking Him, and the trials of providing for our family, God consistently provided for our needs.

13

PARALYZED

One weekend, Cheri went to babysit for a friend's children. As she came down the stairs of their two-story home, her socked foot slid off the top stair and she landed on her bottom halfway down the stairs. Unable to breathe freely or move, an ambulance was called for her and we were summoned to the emergency room of St. Agnes Hospital.

After examining our daughter, the doctor presented us with the grave news: "I fear your daughter is permanently paralyzed from the waist down." Our beautiful, 21-year-old daughter may never walk again? We began to plead with God. As prayers went up, the answer came down. God healed her completely! Miraculously, she was made whole!

14

AND THEN HE WAS GONE

Our family began attending another church, but it just wasn't fulfilling to merely sit in the congregation when you are called to be a shepherd. I was miserable. It would get more miserable yet.

One day while I was at McDonald's doing lunch duty, my boss sent me to the office to receive an important phone call. The police officer informed me that my husband had just been arrested and when I came to the police department he would explain the circumstances to me. Numbly, I finished the lunch duty and called Kings Canyon District Transportation to excuse my absence that afternoon.

When I arrived at the police department, they asked me to have a seat in the lobby. I sat for what seemed to be an eternity but it was all part of God's timing. Our middle daughter, Michele, had become engaged to Kenny while attending Fresno Pacific Bible College. Wesley and Kenny were working on a construction job together when the police arrested Wesley. The delay allowed Kenny enough time to pack up their tools and arrive at the police station just before the officer broke the shocking news to me. The lieutenant explained to me that my husband had just confessed to multiple counts of molesting our former foster daughters about ten years earlier. I felt my knees go weak and Kenny held me up. I began to sob. I don't believe I could have cried any harder if they had told me Wesley had died.

In the following weeks I felt embarrassed to go out in public. I was sure everyone knew what my husband had done and was staring at me. The children and I changed churches and went to a nearby town where we hoped no one would know us. Years later, I realized that hardly anyone made the connection from Wesley's picture in the paper to me or the children. I was being tormented by lies from the enemy.

Life became very difficult. Wesley was there when I left that morning and gone forever that evening. I cried myself to sleep at night missing him and agonizing over what he had done. I had to adjust to one income and being a single parent. One person added to my misery by asking me how I didn't know that he had molested the children. I felt the remark was very accusatory.

Just as I was adjusting to his arrest and being alone after twenty-four years of marriage, I had to endure Wesley's trial. The judge sentenced him to thirty-eight years without possibility of parole. Then they sent him away to Calpatria State Prison, a 10-hour drive from our home. I felt as if the judge had also sentenced me to thirty-eight years... thirty-eight years of being alone and working hard to support the kids while running the house by myself. When there is sin in a spouse's life, the entire family suffers.

15

HOME INVASION

The master bedroom was on the main floor of the farmhouse and the children's bedrooms were upstairs. The home had a staircase inside with an additional staircase on the back of the house. One evening, Cheri and Diane went out on a double date while Michele was in Bakersfield with her fiancé Kenny. At bedtime, Debbie, who was now sixteen, went up to bed alone. A short time later she awoke to find a young man straddling her with his hand over her mouth. She bit his hand and God enabled her to fight off her assailant. I am thankful he did not strike her or molest her but instead chose to flee. We called the police who remained at our home until 3:30 a.m. Debbie was shaken up but unharmed, praise the Lord, our protector.

While we were adjusting to all of this, the next blow hit us. My wages were garnished for Wesley's unpaid debt. I was not even given an opportunity to make payments. The garnishment left me with $550 as our total monthly income from my two jobs. I was already working forty-eight hours a week, there was nothing more I could do. In my panic, I ran to the Welfare Department and asked for assistance instead of running to God for help like I should have done. The lady at the Welfare Department was kind but stated the rules would not allow her to help me because a garnishment was a bill of our creating. It didn't matter that I paid all my *own* debts on time, this was now *my* debt. She went on to explain that if I quit both of my jobs, then they could assist me. Quitting my jobs would accomplish nothing since the debt would remain and I would have to pay it with interest whenever I returned to a job. I returned home totally frightened. How could we live on only $550 a month for the next three months?

With my back to the wall like the children of Israel at the Red Sea, and nowhere to turn, I cried out, "Lord, help me... PLEASE." God in his lovingkindness didn't scold me and say something like, "You thought you could handle this; go ahead." No, instead, He loved me and gave me a plan of action.

Behind our home was a large barn full of Wesley's contractor's tools. God reminded me that with a 38-year sentence Wesley would never use the tools again. The plan? Have a yard sale and sell all the tools. I wrote to him and explained the dilemma. He responded with an apology for having put the family in such a mess and enclosed a list of all the tools and the price they should bring.

A few days later, I received the pricing guide and headed down the long driveway to the barn. I stopped in my tracks and began to crumble. "God, I can't do this," I cried out as I began to weep. To this day I am not sure why I felt so overwhelmed. I know it wasn't the work involved. I'm not sure if it was that I suddenly realized that Wesley was not ever coming home or if it was the thought of dickering with men over prices.

God knew I would need help. Just at that moment I felt two strong arms wrap around me from behind as Kenny gently asked, "What's the matter, Mom?" God had put it in Kenny's heart to come up to spend the weekend with Michele. I knew it was God's timing for Kenny to arrive just when I needed him because he had left his home in Bakersfield an hour and a half before my need.

My daughters and Kenny assisted me in setting up the tool sale and God sent the buyers. Kenny and my girls did all the dickering for me and God gave us $650 in sales that weekend! Our needs were being met by God's mighty hand.

I continued to work six days a week, five school bus driving and McDonald's lunches, and then six to ten hours on Saturdays at McDonald's. On weekends there was also all the duties of a typical single mom: cleaning, laundry, groceries to purchase, a large acre yard to tend and, and, and. All of this work, piled on top of the stress of the trial and garnishment, brought me to the breaking point.

I was driving my bus one morning while tears flowed down my face from behind my sunglasses. I kept wiping them, not wanting my students to see me cry, but more tears immediately took their place. I felt my heart breaking and emotionally I didn't have the strength to make it through another day. I cried out to the Lord, "If you don't help me, I can't make it through this day."

Almost immediately the Lord comforted me by flooding my mind with the words and music for a country-western tune. I had never written a song before and I didn't care for western music, so I definitely knew it was God. The words came so quickly I could scarcely pen them. I drove to my next bus stop and wrote a line, then continued to another stop and wrote the next one. Before I knew it, I had a song, *Loved and Protected.*

LOVED AND PROTECTED

Sometimes I feel so all alone
Abandoned, rejected.
Sometimes I feel my hope's all gone
Abandoned, rejected.
Then I hear my sweet Savior saying,
My darling daughter be not afraid,
I'll never leave you
Abandoned or rejected.

Then I spend a little time in the Word of God
Read I'm loved and protected.
Spend a little time on my knees in prayer
Hear I'm loved and protected.
Listen to the voice of my Savior saying
My darling daughter be not afraid,
I'll never leave you
You'll always be
Loved and protected.

I felt His peace, joy, and a new strength flow into me. I received the refreshing I so needed that day. As I parked my bus and walked over to start my shift at McDonald's, I had a new song and lightness in my heart. I had received the joy of the Lord. Now a second song broke forth from my heart...

I'VE GOT THE JOY OF THE LORD

Now, I've got the joy of the Lord in my spirit,
I've got the joy of the Lord in my heart.
I've got the joy of the Lord bubbling over,
Jesus the joy of my life.

He is my light and my salvation.
He gives me strength when no one else can.
There is none other like my Jesus;
He is the one that I love.
YES, He is the one... that I love!

Only Jesus could comfort me the way He did that day. As I penned His love song to me I felt all my heaviness melt away and His strength pour in like a refreshing wave. Minutes later, as I walked to McDonald's, His joy poured out of me as I wrote this second song about my love for Him.

QUICK, CALL A PLUMBER!

A nother day as I was showering. I had soap from head to toe when I realized the water was gathering at my ankles and was not going down the drain. If I continued to rinse my hair and body it would overflow the floorpan and I would have a big mess on my hands. So, remembering that the Bible says that God would be my husband, I prayed a simple prayer. "God, if my husband were here I would call to him to bring a plunger. But he is not here so I ask You to do for me what a husband would do. I need Your help Lord."

Immediately the drain burped a bubble of air and the four inches of water began to spiral out from around my ankles.

You might think that was just a coincidence, but just a few days later He answered a similar prayer. As I prepared dinner, I made the mistake of putting too many potato peelings down the garbage disposal at one time. When I turned on the disposal, it hummed. I prayed the same prayer: "Lord, my Husband, I need Your help." Immediately the disposal stopped humming and began to chew up its meal. God, the Almighty creator of the universe, didn't have to do these two trivial things for me but I believe He did them to teach me that I was indeed *loved and protected* and to depend on Him for all my needs because He can take care of anything I face. We need to realize He loves us and He is not too busy to meet, not just our major needs, but our small needs too.

KAIROS OUTSIDE

There is a beautiful organization called Kairos Outside. They contacted me and invited me to be their guest for a weekend away with other prisoners' wives. During the weekend their goal was to provide us rest and spiritual refreshing. They pampered us with good food and speakers who offered words of encouragement. Life gets heavy as a wife of a prisoner because although you haven't done anything wrong, you are left to carry the whole load without any of the child support or alimony that a divorced woman would receive.

At one activity we were asked to draw or write something that would show the rest of the group how we were feeling at that point in time. I picked up a piece of yellow construction paper and a piece of black and taped them back to back. When it was my turn to share, I turned the black side toward the group and explained: "Right now all I see is dark like someone pulled a blackout shade down over my life. I know the sunshine is there and someday the shade will rise and then I will see the light shine once again." Then I turned the paper with the yellow side toward the audience.

While we were still in bed one morning, we awoke to the sound of strolling guitar players singing as all the staff came in with bunches of flowers, placing them on our bedcovers along with many notes and poems of encouragement. We felt so much love from these caring people. I thank God for them. I left the weekend feeling very refreshed and encouraged.

Another group I am thankful for is Angel Tree. This organization asks donors to provide gifts for a child of a prisoner and then they are delivered at Christmastime. I cried as the gifts were brought to our home. These gifts of love blessed my children tremendously.

Now it was my turn to help another prisoner's wife find comfort. At a church retreat I felt God prompt me to go outside during the song service. There, sitting on a bench under the beautiful pine trees, I could see an older woman who was crying. I approached her to see if I could pray with her about something. God led me to her because she disclosed to me that her husband had just been found guilty of child molestation! Through her tears she shared thoughts of self doubts that her being old and undesirable was the underlying cause of her husband raping those children. When I shared that my husband too was serving time for molestations, she expressed shock. "But, you are still young and pretty," she declared. As we continued talking and praying together, God brought her release from the guilt Satan had placed on her and she left the retreat with new peace.

18

"I DO"

While we were still living on $550 a month because of the garnishment, it was time to start planning Michele's wedding. As most of you know, the dress can be one of the most expensive details of the wedding. By now, my faith had grown and I had learned to depend on God for everything. I asked the Lord, "How are we going to pull this off?" One day, Michele's older sister generously offered the solution to the problem of the dress.

A year earlier, Cheri was pregnant out of wedlock. She asked us to go with her to buy a dress and, not willing to drive a wedge between us, her sisters and I went along. We found a beautiful dress that day. Cheri paid for it and brought it home. In the meanwhile, I bombarded Heaven with my prayers. I begged God to move in Cheri's life to prevent this marriage, as he was not a Christian. God heard my prayers. Cheri kept her adorable baby boy but broke the engagement. The dress hung in the closet, unaltered and forgotten.

Cheri offered the dress to Michele and it fit her beautifully, not one alteration needed. We sent the dress to the cleaners and for $25 they freshened it and it was ready to go. Michele wasn't just settling, she had loved the dress the day Cheri purchased it. She looked gorgeous in it. The mermaid-style torso of the dress was so flattering as it accentuated Michele's tiny size-eight frame, then broke into mounds of organza ruffles all the way to the floor and down the generous train. With her beautiful blonde curls down her back veiled lightly, she was a breathtaking bride.

Windsor School Reception Hall is an ideal location for a wedding. The historic building is beautiful with its interior stairs stretching from one side of the room to the other as they ascend up to the platform. Massive gilded columns coupled with deep rose-colored velvet drapes, which were held back by golden braided cords, completed the grand appearance. Two tall candelabras and huge standing baskets of flowers were all we needed to add to create a lovely setting for a wedding.

The bakery created a delightful wedding cake by placing a fountain in the center of four round pink champagne cakes that supported the top tier and mountains of cascading delicate pink flowers.

One day I noticed Michele was a little down, which was contrary to her sunny disposition. Michele was concerned that her guests were only going to be served cake at the reception. I reassured her that all of our guests knew our situation and would be fine with just cake. Michele's loving Heavenly Father cared about His little girl and began to move hearts to meet the need.

A couple of days later, I received a surprising phone call. A man from the new church we attended offered to provide a sit-down dinner for the wedding free of charge! He said that morning as he prayed God spoke to his heart to bless Michele with the meal. The men's group was going to buy and prepare the food, supply the dishes, serve as waiters and the cleanup team. Michele's Heavenly Father saw the desire of Michele's heart and provided the dinner for her that her earthly father couldn't. God's Word says that He is a "father to the fatherless" (Psalms 68:5). God showed her it was true.

A NEW DILEMMA

A few days prior to the wedding Kenny approached me. He said he had something to share with me and that he was afraid it would cause me to withdraw my consent for him to marry Michele. I thought, *Oh no, what is he going to share?* Kenny then told me he had been laid off from his job in Bakersfield. I sighed with relief, so grateful that it was a minor thing and not something much heavier. I explained to him that Michele and he could use the upstairs apartment until they were able to move on.

The home we were renting was a large farmhouse owned by the Mennonite church. Within the upstairs there was a second kitchen and a small living room, as well as the two bedrooms they had created to house missionaries when they came home on furlough. We were only using one of the upstairs bedrooms. The kitchen, living room, and one bedroom were not in use, so Michele and Kenny could utilize them as their first apartment. It is not a young man's dream to live with his mother-in-law but it was a great temporary solution to their dilemma. Fortunately, Kenny and I got along well and I enjoyed their company.

At the wedding reception Kenny sat across the table from a guest who had come from San Jose. The guest told Kenny of a job in our area that was available. Kenny applied a couple of days later and got the position. I have always wondered how someone from four hours away knew about a job near us. God provides our needs in marvelous ways; His resources are limitless.

Michele and Kenny moved into the upstairs apartment and Kenny began his new job. It was a blessing to them to help them get on their feet, but it was also a comfort and blessing to me to have a man in the house again. A little time went by and the couple were financially able to secure a place of their own.

A NEW ROOMMATE

One of my Christian co-workers, Martha, came to work one morning visibly upset. When I inquired, she said her roommate was getting married and she couldn't afford to continue to live where she was without half of the rent being covered. Martha didn't know what she was going to do. I asked her to pray with me because I thought I knew the solution.

The apartment upstairs was now empty. I asked the Lord if I should rent it to her. I had finally learned to seek God's wisdom before making life choices. I felt the Lord's assurance that having Martha move in with me was His solution to both her need and mine. Martha moved in and God graciously met both of our financial needs.

The van Wesley had used as a carpenter gave out on us. It was inconvenient but I was able to walk the mile to work so we were alright, with the exception of not being able to drive to church. One of the young women in the church bought herself a new car so she graciously offered me her 14-year-old car. It was old but in good repair and it was a blessing to have wheels again.

WHAT AN ADVENTURE!

A year after Wesley was arrested, I filed for divorce. I didn't hate him, I just couldn't deal with the letdown of my husband, *my pastor,* betraying my trust and molesting children. As I said, I didn't hate him, the pain just ran so very deep.

My two youngest children, Debbie now seventeen and Billy age eleven, wanted to see their father. I had promised them that until they were able to go by themselves, I would take them for visits. What I didn't realize at the time of the promise was the prison would be located ten hours away. The children had not seen their father for over a year due to finances, the distance, and the broken-down van.

As a swing manager at McDonald's, I had accrued a paid week of vacation time and, being summer time, I was off duty as a bus driver. We decided to drive to Calpatria for my vacation and do some fun things along the way.

The night before we left on vacation, my boss called and asked me a favor. He had a survey that had to be done immediately and none of his other managers were willing to tackle it for him. He said it would only take a couple of hours and if I would do it, my daughter, Debbie, could assist me and we would both be paid cash. I don't remember the exact amount but it was quite a bit of money. Debbie and I agreed, completed the task, and pocketed the extra spending money for our trip!

The next morning we headed off in our newly-acquired 14-year-old car. The first stop on our much-needed vacation was Magic Mountain amusement park. Debbie, Billy, and I enjoyed the day riding the rides and actually were some of the last people out of the park. As we walked across the parking lot I found a small wad of money. There on the ground was $17.00 and no one around to whom I could return it. We went on our way to the motel and got a good night's rest.

The following morning we drove to the San Bernardino area to visit a friend from the Orange Cove church. She treated us to a day at the beach and then a lovely dinner with family. It was such a joy to see her again after all those years and to be able to totally relax at the beach after such a trying year.

The next morning as we left her home she slipped $100 into my hand. I protested, telling her we had sufficient money for the trip but she insisted, saying that God had laid it on her heart. I had vacation money, survey money, the $17.00 I found, and now this $100 extra. God was blessing us financially at every turn. Then...

STRANGER WITH A MACHETE

We left my friend's home in the early morning because we needed to cross the desert near Barstow and we had no air conditioning. As we drove south on the highway we saw very few cars. All of a sudden, I heard a loud boom and steam began to pour out from under the hood of our car. Upon investigation we discovered an enormous hole in the radiator hose. I prayed for the Lord's help. I had no cell phone and no towing insurance. It was late afternoon and I dreaded being stranded all night in such an isolated place with my two children.

Within minutes a car came by and pulled over. Two Mexican men got out and came to my car. With extremely little English they asked if they could help. One of the men looked under the hood then went to his car and returned with a machete from under the front seat. I was terrified! He went straight to the hood of the car, grabbed the radiator hose, and with one fluid movement he cut off the blown-out area. He re-attached the hose and made a motion for me to start the car. As soon as I turned the key we heard the most awful noise. "Bad, very bad," he remarked. I knew that too.

In broken English he offered a ride for the children and me into Brawley, a town sixty minutes away. He went back to his car and returned with a tow bar. How many people carry a tow bar in their trunk? God sent them our way just when we needed them! God constantly amazes me with the way He provides. The man hooked the tow bar up to my car and then placed the machete back under the front seat of his car. I was petrified to get in with these two strangers but we really had no option. With great fear we got into the back seat.

As we drove the two men spoke in Spanish and would laugh. I knew nothing about what they were saying. All I knew was we were in the middle of nowhere with two men, a machete and many dirt roads off the main road that went through the desert as far as the eye could see. My fear ran wild. I thought, *What if they turn off on one of these dirt roads? We will be goners—raped, murdered.* Fear is a terrible thing.

To my relief, an hour later we pulled into Brawley, our destination. I asked the men to please put our car at the gas station that advertised a mechanic worked on the premises during the day. There was a whole row of motels across the street so it was my intention to rent a room for the night and deal with the car in the morning. I tried to pay the men for towing us but they refused payment. Finally I was able to get them to take $20.00, so little for a 60-mile tow. The men were so sweet, they handed me a business card and told me in extremely broken English to call if I needed more help and they would drive back up from Mexico to assist us. I felt foolish to have been so afraid of such kind men.

When we looked across the street we had our choice of four motels. Debbie and I both liked the looks of the same motel so we rented a room there. Once in the room I called a local church and asked if they knew a mechanic I could trust. Within their congregation was a mechanic who came over to look at my poor car. After listening to the motor, the mechanic's recommendation was to sell the 14- year-old car to him for parts. He paid me $100.00.

It was almost funny. I had vacation money, the $100.00 my friend gave me, and now another $100.00 from the sale of the car, but no car to go anywhere.

We were within half an hour of the prison but no way to get there. Then I remembered in Fresno I had attended a prisoners' wives fellowship and met a lady there who moved closer to the prison to be able to visit her husband more frequently. I got her phone number from Information and made a call to her home. Her daughter answered the phone and informed me that her mom had already left to go visit her husband. She was going to spend the night in Brawley and then go early the next day to the prison. I was so surprised. *We were in Brawley!* I asked her which motel her mom was staying in, and to my amazement, she was in the same motel we were in—only two doors away!

I called her room and she was more than willing to give us a ride to the prison. Having her by my side made the day so much easier, since she was experienced with the procedures of visiting an inmate.

We had to leave the motel at 3:00 a.m. to be outside the prison before 4:00 a.m. This is something I would not have been aware of. The cars form a long line outside the prison gates and wait for the prison to open at 9:00 a.m. If you are not one of the first cars in line, you spend all your visitation time waiting to get in. Without my guide we probably would have gotten into the prison after lunch, resulting in a very short visit for the children and their dad.

When it was our turn to approach the guard, he sent my son out to the visitor's trailer to borrow a shirt because he had innocently worn a gang color. I was thankful for the loan; otherwise, the visit would have been canceled. We approached the desk once again and were told to remove our shoes and belts and place them on the desk. As I passed through the metal detector the alarm went off. I was handed a razor blade and sent to the ladies' room to remove the underwires in my bra. Placing the wires and razor blade on the desk, I walked through the metal detector once again. This time I cleared it.

Now we entered through a large metal door which clanged shut behind us. We were prisoners between two closed doors—what a terrible feeling. When the door in front of us opened, I felt relief. We stepped out into a large walk area. Above our heads were guard towers with cameras and guards with guns watching our every move. Behind us were heavy metal chain-link fences with rows of coiled barbed wire on top of them. It was a frightful experience. We walked along the sidewalk past building after building until we finally found the one housing my former husband. After checking in with that guard, we were told to take a seat at one of the round tables in the visiting area. This area was a little more inviting, as there are vending machines and table games available.

An hour later, Wesley finally came through the door and the children could begin their much-awaited visit. After their visit with their dad, my friend drove us back to the motel. It was Saturday night, so I called the church again and asked if we could obtain a ride to church the next day. The mechanic and his family cheerfully offered to give us a ride.

Following church, we went to the pizza shop across from our motel and then decided to go for a swim in the motel pool. As my children swam, I visited with another mom. I shared with her our dilemma and how we were stranded, explaining we would probably have to take the bus the next day to return home. God did yet another miracle. The lady then offered us a ride in her van to our door! She and her son had come to visit her husband at the prison and were going back home Monday. They had plenty of room in the van and she would welcome adult conversation for the long drive home. Their home was just thirty miles north of ours so it was not even out of her way to drop us off. I offered to pay for all the gas but she would only take half. God gave us a wonderful week away. It was a time to relax and be refreshed and to see God's mighty hand of love and miraculous provision in action. Everything fit together so perfectly, much like when you weave the fingers of one of your hands in between your other hand. God is *so* good.

Now we were home again but I was back to walking everywhere. I went to the bank and was able to obtain a loan to buy a car with small monthly payments. God blessed me with a little Horizon. It ran well and was economical to operate.

20

A HANDSOME COWBOY

My good friend Leonor and I were both very lonely because the churches in our small town didn't offer any activities for single people. In Sunday School the husbands sat with their arms around their wives and then made plans to go out to eat after church with other couples. I know it wasn't intentional but it just made our singleness more painful. One day, Leonor asked me if I would like to go with her to a singles evening to play volleyball at a large church in Fresno. The next Tuesday we went to check it out. When we walked into the gym and saw about sixty other singles, it brought healing to my heart. Having been in a small town and not finding any other singles had left me feeling that I was the only one going through the misery of divorce and singleness. We began to attend every week and it was there that I met Michael, a tall, ruggedly good-looking 44-year-old man with reddish-brown hair and a mustache. Michael only needed to don a cowboy hat and he would have looked perfectly in place in a western movie.

Leonor had a little girl, Raquel, about nine years old who went with us to volleyball. Raquel saw another girl her age named Jessica and they began to play together. After volleyball, Michael, who was Jessica's father, asked if we would like to join them for ice cream.

At the ice cream parlor, the girls became fast friends. Michael asked Leonor if Raquel could come for a swim play date in his backyard pool and to bring me and my son Billy, who was ten. We enjoyed many Saturdays swimming, playing table games and sharing a meal together. Then, to my surprise, Michael asked Billy and me to go with him and Jessica to an amusement park. On the log ride, Michael sat behind me and wrapped his arms around my waist. As I leaned back against his chest, it felt so wonderful to be cuddled once again. It was a delightful day and the beginning of our courtship.

Saturday after Saturday we would drive to Fresno and enjoy Michael's hospitality, and during the week Michael would drive to my home in Reedley to spend hours getting to know me.

One night as we sat on my front porch talking, Michael began to talk about me moving into his house. After a time, I let him know that I didn't believe in living together. He quickly replied that neither did he and then with a twinkle in his eye he added, "I meant after we are married. Didn't I ask you?"

"No," I responded.

His romantic proposal was, "Oh. Well, then will you?" Then without missing a beat or waiting for my "yes" he continued on with his "moving-in plans." A proposal couldn't get much more romantic than that!

Since this was my second wedding, I did not want a traditional wedding gown. I found a beautiful white knee-length suit that had a high collar with a cutout in the neck and an attached teardrop pearl to dangle from the collar. It had brocaded flowers on the white-on-white fabric, perfect for a second wedding. My father walked me down the aisle, then stepped up on the platform to perform the ceremony.

Michael and his father had not spoken for over ten years. I encouraged Michael to invite his father and stepmother to attend our wedding, and to my surprise they agreed to come. After traveling from Illinois, Michael put his dad and stepmother up at his home. During the next couple of days, old issues were partially resolved and their relationship was restored. What a blessing.

Since Michael's parents could only stay a few days, Michael invited them to stay in his home. On our wedding night, Michael's home housed his mom and dad, my son Billy, Michael, and me. Michael's daughter had decided to spend the night in Reedley at Leonor's home with her daughter Raquel.

About midnight, we had just said goodnight to his mom and dad and were finally headed to bed when the phone rang. Jessica was crying, homesick. We donned our clothes and made an hour's round trip to retrieve our little one.

The next morning, my whole family decided to surprise us with breakfast, and thus our married life began. We never did get to live alone as husband and wife, as later my parents moved in with us, too. It reminded me of the movie "Yours Mine and Ours."

STORMS AHEAD

After the wedding, Michael and I continued to attend church, but Michael was only going through the motions. He no longer attended with enthusiasm. He also began to watch programs on cable TV that were raw and unbecoming to a Christian. Michael stopped hiding his vulgar vocabulary; he was not the man I thought I married. I had been so lonely I only dated Michael a few months before I agreed to marry him. During that brief courtship it was easy for him to put up a good front and pose as a godly man. If I had taken more time to date him, I would have gotten to know the real man. However, I know despite all the pain that was to follow, it was God's plan for me to marry Michael.

It was necessary for me to get up at 4:30 a.m. to go to work. In order to get enough rest I would go to bed at 9:00 p.m. I would wake up at midnight or later and realize Michael still was not in bed. When I would go downstairs to look for him, he was gone. I sat up night after night, crying and praying, wondering where my husband was at those wee hours of the night. When I called his cell phone he would not answer, and yet when he returned home he would say he had just gone out for a drive. Sometimes hours would go by before he returned home, and when he finally came in he would be angry and resentful if I asked where he had been. The arguing became more and more intense and he would shout at me and use his stomach to push me across the room. I knew in my heart of hearts that he was not being faithful and the pain went deep.

On one visit to Michael's mother, he put his cell phone on the charger and then went to take a nap. His phone began to ring and as I lifted it to answer the call, he ran across the room and grabbed the phone from my hand. He then took the phone outside to converse. I watched through the window. His face lit up and I could see him laugh. When he came back in, he placed the phone back on the charger and went to finish his nap.

After he was asleep, I checked the phone number and it was the same one that was on our telephone bill many times a day. I had had enough! I took the phone outside and dialed the number. A woman answered—Patricia. I asked her if she knew Michael was married and she responded that she did. I asked her to leave my husband alone to which she responded, "I can have Michael anytime I want him, he's been chasing me for years." Michael and I worked through that day and I forgave him but the pain still went deep.

At home, Michael turned off his phone in the evenings. I noticed new numbers appeared on the phone bill for lengthy periods of time and several times a day. I knew he was seeing several other women. God spoke to my heart to "Be still and know that He is God," so I prayed and did not confront him. It was not easy but it was a lesson in trusting God to take care of what I could not.

One day, I came home from work and found a pair of panties on the floor of our master bath. Michael tried to tell me that Patricia stopped by while he was working on the car and that he had just let her borrow our shower. Since she lived in town, that was a really lame justification.

My son and I moved out to an apartment. The timing was perfect. I had just received a bonus check which, combined with my regular pay check, was exactly what I needed to pay all the move-in costs. It was a comfortable apartment with a lovely garden of flowers outside my sliding door and a quiet pool just beyond that was used so seldomly by anyone else it felt like it was our own. It was so peaceful, I could gain the rest I needed. I continued to seek God for Michael and for my marriage. I loved Michael but could not endure any more of the pain that I had been coping with for eight long years. Billy and I lived in the apartment together for six months and my spirit received rest from the battle.

Michael's behavior caused me to draw even closer to the Lord as I searched the Bible for comforting Scripture and cried out to God in intercessory prayer for him. I began to sense God telling me to fast as I prayed for Michael. Fasting was a new spiritual discipline for me. The first times I fasted, I skipped eating from the time I got up at 4:30 am until lunch at noon. Going without food for those seven and a half hours was really difficult at first, but I began to notice that when I fasted even that long I felt stronger in my spirit and I was able to deal with Michael's indiscretions easier.

Little by little, God was teaching me to fast for longer and longer periods of time. God now asked me to go on a total fast for a lengthy number of days to pray for Michael, and God enabled me to do it. I learned that fasting not only made me stronger but I was seeing more answers to my prayers. When we combine fasting with prayer, chains fall off our loved ones. God assured me, "I will deal with Michael like a father does a son."

Michael asked me if I would see a marriage counselor with him. I was pleased that he wanted to mend our relationship so I agreed to go. After six months of counseling, we reconciled and I moved home. I wish I could say things changed but, unfortunately, they did not yet.

The enemy again tried to torment me. However, this time it backfired on him. I had been fasting for three days and I felt spiritually strong when the attack came. My phone rang and the voice asked me if I knew where my husband was. To her surprise I answered, "Yes, I know, he is out with another woman." She was shocked. She had called to inform me that Michael was out with her cousin. I believe she was disappointed that I wasn't shocked. God had given me the "peace that passes all understanding." I stood on God's promise to me that "He would deal with Michael as a father does his son."

The church we had been attending closed its doors due to tight finances. At this time Michael was still attending only Sunday mornings and couldn't wait for the service to be over. He wanted nothing to do with the social events. The church's closing caused us to look for a new church home. We visited a church that was comprised of former drug addicts and bikers with lots of tattoos. Having grown up so sheltered I did not feel comfortable there at all, but Michael loved it and chose it as our new church home.

Pastor Tim preached a straightforward message from the Word and men gravitated toward him because he was so real and transparent with them. Pastor Tim told the men that they couldn't "flip skirts on Friday night and be pleasing to God." I began to see some changes in Michael. He was still going out nights but he began to listen more intently to the sermons and attend church more. We began counseling under Pastor Tim and his wife and finally Michael broke and confessed his affairs. God had brought the breakthrough!!! It had been fourteen years of heartache and sorrows but God triumphed, and the joy I experienced seeing my husband serving God made it all worthwhile.

Michael began to change so rapidly. He now attended church every time the doors were open. He became tender toward me and planned dates. Michael and I drew so close to each other and to our God. Michael loved everyone he met and began to reach out to people in need. If anyone needed a bed or refrigerator, he would track one down for them and deliver it. He now truly loved people and his God.

PACKED WITH GAUZE

I woke one morning with a sore spot in the upper-area of my right armpit. Upon investigation I discovered a lump the size of a pea. Just three days later the lump had grown to the size of a walnut and was causing sharp pains to shoot all the way down to my wrist. Fearing it was a fast-growing cancer, my doctor scheduled me for surgery the very next week.

Following the surgery there was more pain as the site had to be left open and packed with gauze for a week. I thank God, however, it was not cancer! Just a month later a similar lump came up under my left armpit. This time instead of going to my doctor, I went to the Great Physician—Jesus. I had Pastor Tim anoint me with oil and pray for my healing. Praise God, it disappeared overnight!

21

RAINY DAY MIRACLE

It was raining as I headed down the two-lane Highway 180 to work early one morning. I began to hydroplane and my car drifted into the lane of oncoming traffic. Two cars were headed toward me as my car sped toward a head-on collision. Once again I screamed, "JESUS!" Immediately my car spun, headed in the opposite direction and then slid off the road as the two cars sped past me. Zoom, zoom, they whizzed by. My car came to a stop along the side of the road just inches from the fence. God caused both cars to miss me and I stopped—not even a scratch on my vehicle. There is such power in the name–JESUS.

22

ENLARGED HOUSEHOLD

My parents, who were now eighty-four years old, lived in Reedley so it was convenient for me to drop in to visit them and help them between bus routes. I took Mom to get her groceries once a week and I noticed that the last week of the month Mom would tell me that she didn't need anything.

When I checked the cabinets and refrigerator, I realized that wasn't the case, so I just started buying her a week's groceries at the end of each month. One day I saw my momma crying. At first she didn't want to share her problem with me but after a little prodding she finally let me know that the apartment manager had raised the rent yet another $50.00 a month. Since they lived on Social Security there was no way they could cover it. I went home and talked to Michael, and we decided to move them in with us.

About six months before, Michael's mother Lucy had planned to move in with us. Her daughter with whom she'd lived had died, and she was all alone. Michael went to work immediately remodeling our two-car garage for her and making it into a bedroom, living room, and kitchenette. Just inside the door from the garage into our house was an existing toilet and sink and the washer/dryer. He added a shower in the laundry room and had created a beautiful apartment for her. Michael was extremely talented; the apartment looked professionally done.

Lucy moved in with us but was so lonely. Lucy was miserable. The combination of grief over her daughter's death and our being gone at work all day overwhelmed her. After a short time she decided to move up north with a couple who were home all day. Her apartment sat empty.

Michael and I agreed that my parents should move in with us. The apartment was ideal for them. The kitchenette allowed Mom the freedom to make breakfast, lunch, and snacks for herself and Dad, and then they joined us for dinner which lightened her load. Mother was a hard worker but her body grew increasingly frail as she battled emphysema and old age. Mother had never smoked but suffered nonetheless from this disease. My heart went out to her as we made many a midnight trip to the emergency room. My mother's prayer was, "Lord, please don't let me die of suffocation."

My momma was a mighty woman of God. I often joined her in their little apartment for prayer. She would sit in her easy chair and I on the carpet at her feet. Mother cupped my hands in her tiny frail hands as we entered the Lord's presence together. What a priceless gift and precious memory.

Mary and Jerry Hough (Mom and Dad)

23

THE "BREAD MAN"

A couple in our church had a ministry of taking bread to the needy. After work Michael and I would go and help them load the trucks with the bread.

One day I came home from work to find Michael was devastated. He had been a victim of downsizing and lost his job. He thought it was the end of the world because he thought, *Who will hire a 62-year-old man?* It was actually a "good" thing (Romans 8:28). Michael had been under tremendous pressure at work and suffered with high blood pressure and diabetes. A few months after his forced retirement all the tension was gone. Michael was joyful and relaxed. We discovered that he could go on Social Security early and it was only $50.00 a month less than if he waited until he was sixty-five. Shortly after Michael lost his job, the other couple gave up the bread ministry and Michael took it over completely. I was still working but I helped Michael load the bread truck after work. Then on holidays and summer months I went out to make deliveries with him. We would start by delivering bread to the homeless and then go to a local motel where the new parolees lived. Michael started delivering bread on Thursdays but the route began to grow and the bakery donated more and more bread until Michael was loading and delivering bread twice a week. He became known as "The Bread Man."

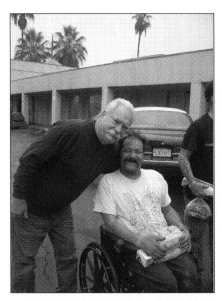

Michael (left) with his new friend (right)

My heart was touched one day when we gave a loaf of bread to a man who rejoiced because "now he had something to put his peanut butter on." He went on to explain to us that someone had given him a jar of peanut butter that morning and he was grateful because the peanut butter was all he had to eat until his first payday next week. Now the peanut butter would become sandwiches.

While Wesley was in prison, he repented of his sin and received God's forgiveness. He began to lead other prisoners to Christ and conduct Bible studies. In time, he became an assistant to the prison chaplain. With such excellent behavior he was given half-time release. The law says that the parolee must return to the county in which the crime was committed, which meant that he would be released to the city of Fresno. When a prisoner is released, they are given $200.00. From that money they have to pay for the clothes they leave the prison with and pay for their own ticket to the court-ordered destination. After paying for these expenses they have very little cash to work with and no job lined up. This is one reason many end up on the streets.

Low income motel—bread recipients

Michael and I paid for a motel room for Wesley immediately after his release. We also took him some used clothes and groceries. As I previously wrote, Michael now loved everyone. The room was in a motel on our bread route, so in the months to come, Michael took bread to Wesley. This was truly a sign of God's work in his life.

Homeless tents

It was while we were delivering to the homeless that we met a man named Donald Anderson. Donald was a likable guy, and over a period of time he asked Michael if he could help him deliver bread. They began to hang out together two or three days a week. Don began to attend church and Bible study with us and was growing in the Lord. As winter approached, we invited Don to come into our home and sleep in the guest bedroom. Don met a lady who attended church with us and they began to date.

One day, Don asked her if he could borrow her van to run a quick errand. When Don failed to return with her vehicle, she called and asked Michael if he would try to find him. Michael located Don but, unfortunately, he was passed out with a needle lying beside him. The police came and arrested Don and he had to serve a year in prison. During the year, his girlfriend and I sent him letters of encouragement and Bible study courses. When his release time came, I sent him dress-out clothes.

Momma's Last Battle

My parents had lived with us for about eight years and Mom's battle with emphysema was becoming more intense. During Christmas break in 2009 we had yet another trip to the emergency room and discovered that she was also battling bronchitis. She was hospitalized and, by the end of Christmas break, they were ready to release her to come home. That presented a problem because she was not strong enough to be home with just Dad to care for her. Dad was in good health but at ninety years old, he was not able to assist her with physically demanding needs and personal hygiene. It was decided to send her to a rehabilitation hospital.

Mom stayed in the rehab hospital for four days and was looking better than I had seen her look for years. She was breathing easily. The doctor said they would be releasing her the next day, after I got off work. I went to work that Friday expecting to pick Mom up in the evening, but life changes in a moment's time.

After I finished the morning route, the boss notified me that I needed to call the rehab hospital. The hospital nurse informed me, "On her way to the shower your mom took a fall and we believe she broke her hip. We have sent her to Saint Agnes Hospital to be checked out." Mom's hip was indeed broken and morphine was not even touching the pain. Mom still kept her faith and remained her sweet little 89-pound self. Between pains she repeatedly quoted, "All things work together for good for those who love God and are the called according to His purpose" (Romans 8:28). When Pastor came to see her, she prayed for him and ministered to him, even though she was in intense pain. That was my momma.

Momma's physician decided to give her Dilaudid, a powerful pain medication. Almost immediately, Momma fell into a peaceful sleep. While she slept, I talked with her physician regarding surgery. He explained to me that with her poor lung condition and age, she was not a good candidate for the operation. The summation of the conversations was not good. All they offered this poor little 89-year-old woman was bed rest with pain meds while the hip healed itself, followed by painful physical therapy. During the night, the Dilaudid caused Mom's vitals to drop so low that it became life-threatening. If they took her off Dilauded, her option was back to morphine. While taking morphine, she screamed in pain. How could she endure days, weeks, or even possibly months of that type of pain? I prayed and then decided to leave her on the Dilaudid. It was the most difficult decision I have ever had to make.

For the next three days, Mom slept in the most peaceful state, not even requiring the assistance of the oxygen tube that had been her constant companion for years. Then, Momma took one final breath and passed ever so gently into the arms of her Savior. Her prayer of "Lord, don't let me die of suffocation" had been answered. Momma passed away January 2010, just three months shy of her 90th birthday.

MORE STORMS AHEAD

A couple of days after his release from the year of imprisonment, Don stopped by the house to visit Michael. We enjoyed breakfast with him while we allowed him to use our washer and dryer to wash the clothes we had stored for him in our storage shed. Don had secured an apartment and Michael helped him take his belongings to his new home. The visit was light-hearted and seemed like old times.

In the weeks to follow, Michael invited Don to return to church but he always had an excuse. A few weeks passed and Don once again stopped by and I made him lunch. We laughed together and Don seemed to be his old self.

My dad was now ninety-one years old and still very healthy. He would walk a mile using a walker for stability, then sit and rest before walking back home again. One day, while sitting out front of a gas station on his walker, he wished people a good day. He had finished his cup of coffee and, after wishing a passerby a good day, the man dropped money into Dad's cup. He quickly explained that he was not panhandling. We all had a good laugh about Dad's new "occupation."

In May 2011, Dad took a really bad fall in the house and had to be hospitalized for a broken back. Two weeks later, while still in the hospital, he contracted MRSA, an acute infection in his blood. We almost lost him. Once he was stabilized, they moved him to a rehabilitation center one mile from our home. That made things a little easier on me. I had been going from home, thirty minutes across town to visit Dad every night, and then home to bed so I could get up at 4:30 a.m. the next morning to do it all over again. I was exhausted.

June 4, 2012 came and I, like so many other school bus drivers, was looking forward to summer vacation... just two more days of school. As I drove to work that morning, I remember it was a very strange day. June in Fresno, California, is typically very hot, usually 100 to 110 degrees. This day it was cold, cold enough to wear a coat and gloomy as if a storm were brewing. Strong gusts of wind were blowing dirt, making it difficult to see the road ahead. I finished the day at work and, as I drove home, entered into a time of prayer and worshipping God. I am so glad I spent that commute time with God because it strengthened me for the horror waiting me at home!

24

KIDNAPPED!

When I arrived at my home, I noticed that the storm had blown our six-foot gate over on top of one of my husband's classic cars. My thought as I approached the door was to alert him to remove the gate, hoping the paint was not severely scratched.

As I entered my home, I heard Donald call to me from the top of the stairs, "Donna, you better come up here and talk some sense into Michael; he broke his finger and won't go to the doctor." Without putting my purse down I ran up the stairs to the bedroom and, not finding Michael there, I stepped into the master bath. Michael was not there, either. Before I could say anything I felt a sharp prick in my back. I whirled around and to my horror, Donald was standing there holding a butcher knife with the handle wrapped in a towel!

He told me that Michael was bound and gagged and he had left him in the garage. I knew Michael had to be hurt because he was not the type of guy to just allow Donald to tie him up. Donald said he and another man had committed a crime and he needed money to get out of town. He took my purse and threw my cell phone across the room. I thought to myself, *Oh no, Dad's money is in my purse.* Dad always wanted me to cash his Social Security check and bring him all cash. In the bottom of my purse was his $1,400.00. I whispered a prayer. God led me to ask Don if I could please have my credentials back so I could drive the bus the next day. Donald handed me my purse and said, "Just give me your money." I reached into my wallet and gave him $16.00 which he quickly rammed into his pocket, without even looking to see how much it was. I had Dad's $1,400.00 back! My first miracle of the day had just occurred!

Donald then told me that the day before, he and another man had committed a crime and that the other man killed someone. He then said I was to drive him to another town where we would meet up with his partner and that when I got home, I could untie Michael. He further instructed me to not indicate to any of the neighbors that there was anything wrong or he would *kill me* and them too. Donald's thoughts seemed disconnected; he was not his usual laid-back, jovial self. It appeared as though he was on some drug.

We got into my little Mustang and I began to drive him south of Fresno for about forty-five minutes. As we drove, we came to a country area with only orchards and vineyards for as far as you could see. I remembered hearing that when a kidnapped victim leaves the place of abduction, they don't usually survive. I was terrified.

Donald added to my fear when he said, "We are going to turn down a long road to a hidden house where a drug dealer lives, and when we get back there don't you dare scream."

"Why, what are you going to do to me?" I sobbed.

"Never mind," he responded gruffly. "Stop crying."

"I can't help it; you're scaring me." At that, I tried to stop the tears and I prayed with all that was within me for God to help me and for His wisdom. I told Donald, "I love you like a brother, Donald. You don't have to do what you are planning. Furthermore, God loves you too and He will forgive you."

Donald replied, "After tonight, you will hate me."

I responded, "I might not like what you have done, but I won't hate you. Please, just let me pull over and you can take my car."

"If I let you go, you will tell the police," he responded.

"You can be long gone before I reach any help, Don. Look at where we are. You took away my cell phone at my house." Miraculously, at that point, he allowed me to pull over and get out of the car.

His final instructions as I grabbed my purse were, "Walk through that vineyard. I'm going to sit here and watch. If you return to this street, *I will kill you*. Walk all the way through, then go to the other road."

As I entered the vineyard, I noticed I was entering at "Row 50." I am grateful that I noticed the row number because later it became very important. I tried to hurry because I was so worried about Michael, but the blustering wind resisted my every effort. The vineyard had just been freshly tilled, so with each step I sank to my ankles in the soft soil. Every step was drudgery. With the combination of stress and the dust blowing in the air, I had an asthma attack. I was grateful to have my inhaler in my purse.

As I persevered, I finally reached an asphalt access road. The walk to the main road past fifty rows of vines would be so much easier now. When at last I reached the main road, I spotted a house about three blocks away. As I approached the house I noticed large piles of dog feces. Fear struck me. I prayed that God would not let me be eaten alive by the large beast. No one was home so I made my way back to the main road.

With no help in sight, I prayed once again. Within minutes I saw a car in the distance. As they approached, I flagged them down and told them that I had been kidnapped.

They called the police and were kind enough to wait with me for half an hour until the police arrived. As we waited they told me they had been looking for a friend's house and couldn't locate it. They were lost and didn't have a clue why they even turned down my road, but I knew.

Finally the police arrived and my hours of interrogation began. During that entire time of questioning, no other cars came down that lonely country road. God had sent that family to rescue me. As the officer questioned me, I was glad God had helped me notice the vineyard row number was fifty. When the detective drove to that location, he was able to verify my story by the car tracks and my footprints in the deep soil.

Eventually we had about six officers on the scene. As each one arrived I asked for any information about Michael. They each reassured me that Fresno officers were at the house and as soon as they could they would pass along news of Michael's status.

I was exhausted and cold, as it was now about 8:00 p.m., three hours after the kidnapping began. I hadn't had dinner yet or been brought out of the field. When the officer put me into his car he said we were heading to Fresno, my hometown. I was grateful, thinking I would finally get to go home and find out if Michael was alright or in the hospital. To my dismay, the ordeal was not over yet. The officers took me to the Police Department to give my official statement to the detective who had been at my home. I had repeatedly given my account to each set of officers who came to the vineyard area and now, one more time.

The officers seated me in a room to wait another agonizing half an hour for the detectives to arrive.

As I waited, I pleaded with the officer, "Please tell me, is my husband in the hospital?"

His response was, "We don't know yet but the detectives will know, and they should be here any time now."

When the detective arrived he introduced himself and asked me to please go into another room with him to answer a few formal questions. I boldly then declared, "I am not going to answer another question for you until you answer one for me. IS MY HUSBAND DEAD?"

"Yes," was his gentle reply.

I was allowed to cry for about ten seconds before the detective gently said, "I know this is difficult but we need your statement so we can catch this guy. Can you pull yourself together and help us?" With that I was whisked away for more questions. Finally at about 10:00 p.m. that night, I was released to the loving arms of my four children and their spouses.

My daughter Michele lived nearby, so she took me to her home where my son Billy and I stayed for the next week. As we all talked, I learned that Billy had started home from work at his usual time, which would have put him at the house about the same time as my abduction. On his way home, Billy had returned to work to retrieve something he had forgotten and, therefore, was delayed in arriving home. I am so thankful God caused the delay because being a well-built 30-year-old, 6-foot-4-inch tall young man, I know Billy would have come to my defense, which might have resulted in his being badly injured or dead also.

When he entered our home, Billy followed a bloody smear on the floor which lead him through two rooms of the house. As he stepped around the corner, there, on the floor, he discovered a rolled up blood-soaked blanket. Fear gripped him as he unrolled the body, not knowing who he was going to find inside. Billy attempted CPR but Michael was already deceased. After calling the police, he too had to undergo a couple of hours of questioning.

We were dealing with police from two cities which complicated things and created several torturous hours before Billy and my daughters were able to receive word that I was fine.

I praise God, too, that I was not injured or killed. Donald had already killed Michael; he had nothing to lose if he had just plunged that knife into my back. I often think how I could have died that night or been horribly injured for life with the size of that blade. I thank God for protecting me and Billy and granting us His supernatural peace. Neither of us has suffered any trauma as an on-going result of the horrors of that night.

I went to meet with the funeral director the following day. Since we didn't have burial insurance and all our money was tied up in classic cars, I had planned to use my credit card. The funeral director suggested that I contact Victims of Violent Crimes. He explained that this organization helps pay the funeral bills of those who were victims of violent crimes. I was so thankful. Not only did they pay $5,000 toward the cost of the funeral but they also gave me $2,000 to move on. What a blessing to have the financial strain removed during this difficult time.

On Friday, June 8th, just four days after my kidnapping, the police found my Mustang abandoned at the edge of Fresno. The tank was almost full. Why did he abandon the car instead of running cross-country? He was already forty minutes south of Fresno. Why had he turned back? The car was not damaged at all and was quickly returned to me. Praise the Lord for that blessing during the storm.

We had Michael's funeral on Saturday to allow his many friends to attend without missing work and his daughter to come from Nevada. The church was packed to the maximum. Michael was loved by so many.

The procession following the hearse to the cemetery must have caused questions to those we passed. Following the hearse was a large group of Michael's biker friends on their Harleys, then Michael's bread truck loaded with bread, my school bus full of my friends from work, and finally the numerous cars. I am sure people we passed wondered, *Who was this guy?*

God gave me and my family supernatural peace to be able to comfort others at the funeral. The day following the funeral was Michael's birthday, so after church I threw a birthday party for him and reminded his guests that Michael was celebrating his first birthday in Heaven.

After staying with my daughter, Michele, for a week, I felt the need to get settled into a place of my own. She and her family had been gracious hosts, but after all that had happened, I just wanted to be alone and quiet. As I drove around looking for a new apartment I asked God to lead me, and He did just that. The first apartment I looked at was perfect: a quiet gated community of single-story units with two bedrooms, washer/dryer hookup and my unit had a twenty by twenty-five foot backyard for my two puppies to play in. Across from my front door was a small grassy area and a large tree, making this unit feel more like a small house rather than an apartment. My son moved in with me and it was a wonderful place to live.

MEDIA

Entering my home, where my husband had been murdered and I had been kidnapped just a week before, was very difficult. God gave Billy and me strength as we began to pack. It was going to be a lengthy process, as I had our large two-story home and my parents' quarters totaling 2,600 square feet to pack up or decide to give away. We were downsizing to 1,000-square-foot apartment and no garage. In addition to the house, there were also two Harleys, seven classic cars, the new two-car garage and two storage sheds full of car parts to find new places for.

The first day or two of packing and moving went well, but then the media discovered we were in the house and tried to obtain interviews, which we declined. Without an interview, in their attempt to keep the story alive, they posted pictures of us moving along with the address and even a map showing where we lived! Every night for the next two weeks our home and storage units were burglarized. Every day when I went to the house to get more work done I would first have to start by filing yet another police report. Twice the house was entered by breaking a window; however, only my dad's wallet and minor things were taken. I then had to deal with identity theft but the bank assisted me and, thank God, the ID theft stopped almost as quickly as it had begun.

The next day they stole our Camero Z-28 off the driveway. Our capable police department was able to recover it within four days and arrest that thief.

The neighbors were watching the front of my house but the back of the home butted up against the home of a drug user, and it was later discovered that it was he and his buddies who were coming over the back fence to rob us. After ten incidents, they were finally caught but not until after they stole my pool pump and all the copper wire that led to the timer, a set of classic tires, many of my husband's tools, a roof of one of the cars and even a 7½-foot satellite dish! The daily onslaught was so draining.

The stolen items were never recovered but at least the thief was apprehended and is serving time. My insurance company paid for some of the items but ruled that all car-related items were not covered. They would only pay for other items as they were replaced, so I received very little insurance money.

Prior to my husband's death, we had lived in that home for nineteen years without a single robbery in the neighborhood.

I felt as if I were a bystander watching a war between the Lord God Almighty and Satan. As evil hit me on one side, God would send me a blessing to offset it. During the two-week siege of robberies, I was simultaneously receiving great blessings.

After the hazard team came in to clean up the blood from the house, there was a good deal of restoration needed. Donald had dragged Michael through three rooms of the house and the police had black fingerprint powder everywhere. The precious men of my church offered to do all the work and the repairs if I paid the $10,000 for the materials. I had no cash that I was aware of, so again, I needed God's help. One of my dad's friends, Don Smith, who was helping me move the classic cars and empty all the parts from the storage areas, offered me $10,000 cash for one of the cars. I had not even let Mr. Smith know my need. God had supplied the beginning monies!

Those precious men worked every night until 11:00 p.m. restoring sheetrock, laying new carpet, replacing the ceiling, and painting the entire inside of the house. One of the workers called a carpet company and obtained carpet for my entire home at cost. The insurance company paid for the downstairs carpet, so my only out-of-pocket expense was the upstairs rooms. Those precious men gave me a bill for their labor and insisted that when the insurance company paid me, I was to keep their earnings. It was after the men left working on the house each night at 11:00 p.m. that the thieves came over the wall to strike again.

Weary from the robberies, I called my church office and asked for help with the move. I had planned to take my time and move gradually, but the robberies no longer made that possible if I wanted to keep my possessions. The church family arrived with multiple trucks and began emptying the house with lightning speed. It was overwhelming dealing with so much all at one time. When we started on Michael's closet, I had an anxiety attack followed with a bad asthma spell. One of the men prayed for me and it lifted. The trucks continued on their missions, one truck to the thrift shop, one to my daughter's house for a yard sale, and one to the apartment.

My apartment bedroom was not large enough to house all of my bedroom suite so we decided to put Michael's tall dresser in my son's room and I would continue to use the long mirrored dresser. As we emptied the tall dresser, we came across a thick sealed envelope. When we opened it, to our surprise there was $8,600! Michael had sold a pickup truck a couple of weeks before his death and stashed the money in his dresser. I hadn't found it in the bank deposits so I was not aware of what had become of it. What a miracle! The night Donald Anderson kidnapped me, he had rummaged through the house looking for cash, and then there were the break-ins, and none of these people found the cash! God had preserved it for me to cover an upcoming need.

After Michael passed away, I went to Social Security and applied for widow's benefits. The worker told me that I didn't qualify because I had made too much that year. Why is it that although that same check was given to us while my husband was alive, I was now supposed to somehow make it without it? *God had a plan!* The money I had just found in Michael's dresser paid the mortgage until the day the house was rented out.

Prior to Michael's death, he asked me to move with him to Nevada. I didn't want to move. All four of my children and eight grandsons live in California and I didn't know anyone except my step-daughter in Nevada. After praying about the matter, God urged me to submit to my husband's request. I still didn't want to go but I had the assurance that it would be alright because God said for me to retire. After Michael's death, I applied for my Social Security widow's monthly benefits and was told that I would not qualify until my retirement. My retirement was in motion at the time of his death so I only had to live on just my school bus income for six months. My submission brought harmony to my marriage and I didn't actually have to move; I only had to be *willing* to do so.

A single mom I knew was crying with pain from a bad toothache. Her dentist wanted $200 to take care of the tooth but she didn't have the needed funds. God spoke to my heart to give it to her even though I had very limited money myself. In obedience, I gave her the $200 to meet her need. The following day, my son attended his church and a young man there gave him a card to bring to me. Inside the card was a check for $500! I didn't even know the young man. I had given God $200 and less than 24 hours later, God gave me $500. It really pays to obey God even when it is difficult.

MORE STORMS BREWING!

The Bible tells us a story about a man named Job. Job was an extremely wealthy man and the father of ten children. In one day's time, Job lost all his wealth and all ten children died. From this example we can learn that when Satan tries to destroy our faith, he hits us with one attack after another trying to take us down. We have to stand firm with God at our side as Job did, and in the end God will reward us with blessing after blessing.

In the storm,
He is with you,
He loves you
and the storm is not
an indication of sin in your life.

Dad had been very sick for three weeks now with his back broken and MRSA, then Michael was murdered, I was abducted, and our home robbed nightly for two weeks, *but that was not the end of the storm.*

Just two weeks after Michael's funeral, on June 4, 2012, Dad took a turn for the worse. For the next thirteen days Dad stopped eating, and I had to endure the pain of watching him slip away day by day. The strain was almost too much to bear. God carried me through those tough weeks. I was at Dad's funeral just one month after I buried my husband.

Once again, God provided for His daughter's need. My dad was a retired minister and his organization sent me a check that covered his funeral expenses. Even in our most trying times, God is there with His ever-present hand holding us up and caring for our every need.

THE TRIAL

Daddy's funeral was on Saturday, July 14, 2012 and on the following Monday we had to be in court for Don's trial. They had captured him when he entered a store. The store owner recognized him from the flyer the police had distributed and notified the police. I've always wondered why he returned to Fresno when he had my car and was already forty-five minutes south of here.

The Victims of Violent Crimes case worker had forewarned us to be prepared for the worst. She warned that murder trials can drag on for years unresolved and the families have to go back time and time again. Our family had prepared a letter for her to read to Don and the court. The letter said that as a family we forgave Don for Michael's murder and that God would forgive him too if he would just ask. The media broadcast that letter on several TV stations and in the newspaper. God received glory.

The court then read part of Don's statement which said he had come to the house that day to kill the entire family, that he enjoyed killing, and couldn't wait to get to prison where there would be plenty of people to kill. He showed no remorse, and since he had pled guilty to all counts, the judge sentenced him that very day! The judge sentenced Don to five and a half consecutive life terms with no possibility of parole for seventy years. Court was miraculously over in only one hour!

NEW MINISTRIES

I received a phone call from one of the residents at the motel where Michael and I had delivered bread. They were having a community potluck and wondered if I would come and share how I got free of my kidnapper and what had happened to their "Breadman." I agreed to come. After I shared and included all the blessings, too, I gave an altar call and one lady accepted Christ.

Summer was over and it was almost time to go back to school bus driving. Just before the new school year began, my boss Luanne called me to see how I was doing. I told her that despite the ordeals, I was doing great because God is my strength. She then asked me if I would like to share my story during our back-to-school meeting. Luanne went on to say she thought it might be easier for me to share once with everyone instead of people asking questions day after day. I readily accepted. For twenty-four years I had lived the life of a Christian in front of my co-workers but now I would have twenty minutes to share the story of God's sustaining grace during our times of trouble. I finished by telling them that if they didn't know Jesus they didn't know what they were missing, because He can bring you joy and strength in the midst of the roughest day.

My retirement paperwork was being processed. It was determined that to receive the maximum benefits, I should retire in December rather than at the end of the 2012/2013 school year. I had such mixed emotions—it would be wonderful not to need to rise at 4:30 a.m. those cold winter months and leave my home in the dark of morning to drive my school bus. However, I would miss all my friends at work and the children I had driven to school since they were in kindergarten. December was busy like every other Christmas season, gifts to buy, many parties to attend, and then my last day of school and my retirement party. I received a handsome plaque indicating my twenty-two plus years of service and many lovely gifts.

January came and it was time to buy a new calendar for 2013. I opened it and stared at all those blank pages. I remember wondering: *What will I do now?* In the past year my life had changed so radically: I was no longer caregiver to my parents, no longer a wife, no longer the keeper of a large-two-story home *and* no longer employed. What would I do now with this majorly unstructured life? I felt lost, alone, and empty.

Then I read in the Bible, Isaiah 41:10, "Fear not for I am with you: neither be thou dismayed; for I am your God: I will strengthen you; yes, I will help you; yes, I will uphold you with the right hand of my righteousness."

THE GREAT I AM WHO:

  - Fed the Israelites for forty years in the desert
  - Who opened the Red Sea so they could walk through
  - Who walked on water
  - Who calmed the sea and healed the sick

Who also rose from His grave, speaking to my spirit: "FEAR NOT FOR I AM WITH YOU! I'VE GOT YOU AND I HAVE GREAT PLANS FOR YOUR LIFE. I'VE GOT YOU BY YOUR HAND AND I WILL LEAD YOU SO DON'T BE AFRAID OF THE FUTURE."

When a child places their hand in their mom or dad's hand, they do not have to be afraid because their parent will lead them where they are going and will protect them and provide for them along the way. Father God assured me: "**I have your hand and we will fill those blank pages together!**"

WIDOW'S SUPPORT GROUP

I had to laugh when some of the elderly widows in the church came to me and asked me to start a widow's support group when I had only been a widow for a few months. What did I know about widowhood? As I prayed about this new ministry, God urged me to begin. Although I was a recent widow I had been in the Word of God all my life, and because of my length of time in the Scripture, I knew verses that were my source of strength and joy and could be theirs, too.

Many of the widows that I ministered to needed a ride to our meetings. I could only pick up one lady at a time because most of them were much older than I and could not climb into the back seat of my Mustang. I felt I was to buy a Toyota Camry, so I began to investigate. All the 2012/13 models I found were around $17,000 and had been driven 50,000 miles or more. God told me, "Now just wait."

I felt I was to put Michael's Harley Road King up for sale at the price it was appraised for by the dealership. At that price, I did not receive even one offer. Several months later a young man from church asked me if he could help me sell the bike. He put the same ad in Craigslist and sold the bike the next day for full asking price. I asked him if he would also help me sell my Mustang and he found a buyer for that in record time, too. Now God assured me it was time for the Camry. This same young man called me the next day and said he had found me a real good deal on a 2011 Camry. The Camry was a salvage car but in excellent repair, and because of the salvage it only had 29,000 miles on it. The young man negotiated for me and with God's favor, the dealer agreed to pay tags, tax and license fees and at a total less than he had originally asked for the car itself! I was able to pay cash using the monies from the sales of the Harley and Mustang with no car payments or DMV fees.

BLESSINGS POURED OUT

After three years in the apartment, I was now ready to move forward with my life. I sold the family home and God blessed me with a lovely 1400-square-foot home that had just been renovated. This home was perfect for Billy and me with its open floor plan and many 82" windows for added lighting. I loved walking into the rooms with their fresh paint and beautiful wood floors. The renovators did not do the landscaping, however, so I have enjoyed my hobby as an amateur gardener deciding each and every flower and shrub to plant. This home is ideally located, too, as it is just two miles from Debbie's home and one mile from Michele's. Cheri lives just forty-five minutes away in another town.

HAITI

During the evenings of 2015, I began to crochet little dolls to place in the shoe boxes that go to Operation Christmas Child, a division of Samaritan's Purse, a ministry of Franklin Graham. As I made the dolls I found myself using dark brown yarn for the legs and bodies of the dolls and adding black yarn braided in corn rows with brightly colored bows at the end of each row for hair.

As I made the dolls, a strong desire came over me to send them to Haiti. I was greatly disappointed to learn that our boxes from California are shipped west, and if I placed the dolls in our boxes they would never go to Haiti. Then, God made a way. A young woman from our church was headed to Haiti on a missionary trip and offered to carry my dolls to Haiti to our church orphanage there! After sending the dolls off with Dorina, I continued working with Operation Christmas Child. In the summers of 2016 and 2017 it was my privilege to go to the Los Angeles area to work for a few days processing the boxes that we and other churches had prepared for distribution.

One of the projects our home church did in preparation for the boxes was to sew gathered material onto the bottom of T-shirts, transforming them into dresses. While sewing some of these dresses, once again my heart's desire was to take them to Haiti. You can only imagine my surprise when I received an e-mail from my church office asking me if I would like to be one of the team members going on a missions trip to Haiti in July 2017! My joy and excitement could hardly be contained!

At 6:45 p.m. we boarded the first of three flights and headed for Haiti. Our trip co-ordinator had ordered our group tickets months earlier and was blessed to receive first-class tickets at the economy class price. God had granted us favor. After making our connection in Los Angeles from Fresno, we enjoyed dinner on the plane. We were then able to settle back in our comfortable first-class seating and get a few hours sleep before landing in Florida. We arrived in Port-Au-Prince about 9:00 a.m. local time. It was then time to travel in our three vehicles on a six-hour trip deep into the mountains of Haiti.

Driving in Haiti is an adventure! Cars, busses, motorcycles, horse-back riders, mules laden with wares for sale, and pedestrians all share both sides of the un-divided road. When a motorcyclist or car comes up behind a group of pedestrians, there is a blast of the horn and everyone scatters.

As we made our way to Pignon, there was a stop at a grocery store. We were advised not to purchase any prepared foods because our delicate American stomachs were not prepared for the bacteria we might ingest. Consequently, an apple became our lunch and we were on our way again.

The first hour the roads were paved and the journey was going smoothly, but then our truck with all our baggage *and* our canned food for the week broke down! Four of us from the truck had to move into the other two vehicles... squish, squeeze! Our driver and his friend stayed behind to take care of the broken-down truck and protect our belongings.

Now, the final hour of our journey. The dirt road ahead was strewn with the biggest pot holes you have ever seen. Our car swerved to and fro, tossing us about like rag dolls as our driver zigged and zagged back and forth, avoiding the other vehicles coming directly at us as they too maneuvered around the potholes. Our driver was amazingly skilled.

Just when we thought the way couldn't get any more unbelievably difficult, our vehicles approached a river and the driver informed us that we had to go through it! Whoa! As we plowed through, we saw people on either side of us bathing and others washing their laundry. We were blessed that the river was low that day. Our driver informed us that the week before he had to wait there for five hours before the waters receded enough for him to cross.

Pignon is a lot like Tijuana with its shacks as homes, fabric as a door, tin roofs and brightly painted rose and teal walls, both colors often together on the same house. They use cactus closely planted together to form their fences and also to double as a clothesline. There is a strange mixture of shacks and tiny businesses next to beautiful two-story homes belonging to the city officials. The people of Pignon spend a lot of time out of doors socializing with one another. All day long the streets are filled with a strange hustle and bustle, very different from the quiet neighborhoods of the United States where we rarely know our next door neighbors.

Market Street on Saturday

Exhausted and extremely hungry, we pulled into the missionary compound. I wondered if we would have dinner since all our food was on the truck we left behind. I was pleased when we came inside the mission home and saw a wonderful dinner prepared for us by the Haitian ladies from the local church. The table was set with a lovely hand-embroidered tablecloth upon which sat colorful plastic plates and glasses. Each of the plates was a different color of bright red, green, blue, or yellow and our plastic glasses were also of the same colors, but not placed by the matching plate. When we entered the room and observed this festive table within the bright yellow walls, we couldn't help but feel joyful. These beautiful ladies had prepared delicious fried chicken, rice, fresh pineapple slices, and mangos for us.

The battery-operated fans we brought with us were on the truck that broke down but God also took care of that need. He caused a storm to blow a cold wind through the house, cooling it and enabling us to be comfortable in this hot, humid climate. We had no clean clothes so we all just dropped into bed in our travel clothes and kissed the world good night.

At daybreak we were awakened to the sounds of cocks crowing and the Haitian men's church choir rehearsing songs of praise in beautiful harmony. What a glorious way to begin a day!

After a huge but unusual breakfast of spaghetti noodles topped with sliced avocado and hard-boiled eggs, mangos, and homemade Haitian bread, we headed down another dirt road to the Fontaine orphanage to visit the children. The potholes were beyond enormous due to the previous night's rain. This orphanage was small, only ten children due to space. The pastor, in mercy for the local children, had converted two closets in the church into sleeping quarters. There were three sets of bunk beds forming a U-shape in each of the tiny rooms, with only two feet of floor space between the beds. They had no window and no fans. My heart went out to them. How hot it must have been at night!

These precious children were so excited to receive a Bible, a dress I had made for each girl, and a new T-shirt for each boy. I had also packed bubbles which these little ones enjoyed for over an hour. It was a blessing to see the smiles on their faces as they received such small gifts. We invited them to attend the Vacation Bible School in Pignon that we were conducting the next day, then bid them farewell with hugs and kisses.

We had three house ladies who cooked breakfast and lunch for us which allowed us more time for ministry. After cooking lunch and tidying up the dishes they would then head home to care for the needs of their own families. The little monetary compensation they requested blessed their families and they blessed us with one delicious meal after another.

Monday morning we awoke at 5:00 a.m. to a breakfast of french toast made from their Haitian bread. It was delicious and an interesting twist on traditional french toast. Their french toast was bread baked in a large square pan, then cut into strips about two inches thick before pan frying it. They served it to us topped with powdered sugar. At every meal we were blessed with all the fresh pineapple, mangos, and avocados we could eat because they are locally grown.

Then it was off to Vacation Bible School. At 8:00 a.m we had 200 children in attendance, but as the morning progressed the crowd grew to 300. It was a difficult morning, as we were training the teen volunteers how to assist us and interpret our Bible lessons. It was an immense blessing as thirty children received Jesus Christ for the first time.

Day 3—1000 kids

The third day of Vacation Bible School was amazing! Word had spread that there were "Blancos" in Pignon and over 1,000 children came to see! They loved to touch our white (blanco) arms and stroke our hair. As we shared the gospel with the standing-room-only crowd, the Holy Spirit moved in their little hearts and over ninety children received Jesus Christ as their savior. The trip to Haiti was so endearing. We were able to plant God's Word in so many children's hearts and feel the love these dear children and adults gave so freely.

We once again loaded the truck with our baggage. In typical Haitian fashion, three teens bummed a ride by hopping on top of the luggage. On our trip to Pignon, we passed one truck loaded so fully that its contents loomed about six feet above the cab. To our horror, many young men were perched atop all that cargo. As this truck made its way down the windy mountainside with its steep embankments, my mother's heart felt fear for the boys' safety. We also passed many motorcycles with five and even six passengers on one bike! Motorized transportation is scarce in Pignon; people grasp at any available mode.

Knowing we had to cross the river once again and that the rain from the night before might have caused it to swell, our trip planners wisely chose for us to drive to Port-au-Prince the evening before our flight. Once again we were blessed: the river was still crossable.

When we arrived at the hotel, the desk clerk informed us that she didn't have our reservation and all of the rooms in our price range were already rented for the night. After showing her our copy of the reservation, she blessed us with an upgrade to suites at no additional cost! Favor again!

All week long in Pignon, ten of us ladies slept in one tiny screened-in porch lined on both sides with metal bunkbeds draped with mosquito netting. Our bathroom was only one sink with a much-too-small mirror and two showers. Now, at the hotel in Port-au-Prince, we had a suite for every two ladies with air conditioning, king-sized beds, and a bathroom of our own. It was a refreshing blessing before our long flight home.

Our sleeping quarters

RESTORATION

Since my trip home, I have continued working with Operation Christmas Child making dresses for the shoe box gifts. I also minister weekly as a greeter on Sunday, a volunteer in our church office, lead a Bible study discussion group, hostess a life group, and conduct a bi-weekly meeting for our widows. I once again feel fulfilled as God has restored my full-time ministry much like I had when Wesley worked in Orange Cove.

Cheri's church ladies' group was taking a cruise in 2013 to Ensenada, Mexico. I was delighted when she called and invited me to go with her because it would be my very first cruise and it was also to be a Bible retreat on board. One afternoon as I stood alone on the deck, all I could see in any direction was water. The words to the song "Oceans" came to mind. I felt the Lord calling me to new areas of trusting Him and, so-to-speak, walking on water. I prayed and asked the Lord to make me a fisher of men.

After returning from crossing the ocean to the east to Haiti in 2017, now a new opportunity to walk on water was presented to me. This time we would cross the ocean twice as far, but west to the Philippines to evangelize for nine days.

EXPANDING MINISTRY TO THE PHILIPPINES

Not too long ago I was looking everywhere for my cell phone and could not find it anywhere. I was mystified. My home is not cluttered and I usually methodically place keys and my phone in one particular place. After I checked everywhere I could think of a second time, I asked my son to dial my number, hoping to hear the ring. *Ring* came the sound from behind me. I whirled around and glanced at the counter. The phone was not there. *Ring* came the sound again from behind me. This time I realized the phone was in my back pocket! After I laughed at myself, I felt the Lord speak to me. "You do not always feel Me near, but I am always as close to you as your cell phone was."

As the day approached for our first Philippines team meeting on April 8, 2018, I began to pray that God would assemble just the right people to form the team He desired. I was introduced to three men, two teenage girls, and another woman. As I continued to pray for unity and God to bless our team, the woman dropped out of the team and another lady joined; then one man was replaced by another man. God was indeed hand-picking our seven-member team.

I was excited about what God would do on that two-week missionary venture because the Philippine government had invited us to enter the individual classrooms of their schools and present the gospel to their children. We were allowed to share the plan of salvation and pray with the children who desired to receive Jesus as their Savior! To make the story clear to the children, we used a marvelous tool called "Evangel Cube." This remarkable cube unfolds in one direction after another opening to four times its beginning size and reveals one picture after another. It shows the children the story of Jesus's death and resurrection. It is a fantastic tool but requires much practice to be able to move skillfully from frame to frame. Practicing our presentation of this cube and learning many other needed things was covered in our two-hour weekly meetings over six weeks to prepare us for the upcoming ministries.

Children praying

In addition to going into the schools, we also spent our days visiting a prison and handing out flyers inviting people to attend the evening open-air concerts, at which time we presented our testimonies and preached. The two Sundays that we were in the Philippines, we attended a different church and asked to be the guest preacher for the morning. Our trip preparation included preparing two sermons.

The months of preparation were finally completed and we were leaving in just two days. Then I heard the news report that a cyclone was headed for Manila the same day we were scheduled to be there! Would our flights be canceled? Would it be safe?

I was greatly concerned. My son and I prayed that God would divert the storm and spare the Filipino people the devastation of yet another storm hitting their land. God heard our prayer and shortly after praying we heard a new report that the storm had turned toward Vietnam. We prayed once again asking God to also spare Vietnam. Soon thereafter, the weatherman announced that the cyclone had turned and was headed out to sea! God had not only spared these precious people, but He had enabled our missions trip to leave as scheduled.

After a three-hour car ride to San Francisco, we boarded the plane for our fourteen hour trip to Manilla. From Manilla, we caught another plane for a one-hour flight to Cauyan, Philippines. However, that flight didn't leave until 7 a.m. the following morning so we got a hotel room and a much needed good night's rest in a bed. Before bed, we visited a McDonald's restaurant and chuckled as we spotted both spaghetti and chicken added to their menu of hamburgers and french fries. Early the next morning we boarded the plane for the last leg of our journey. When we arrived in Cauyan, we paused long enough to place our belongings in a modest hotel room before immediately leaving for our first missionary outreach, the first of ten open-air meetings. It was amazing: following the sermon, an invitation was given and several hundred people came forward to receive Jesus as their Savior! Tired in body but joyful in spirit we headed back to our rooms for a comfortable night's rest.

Missionary house

The rooms were very humble but extremely clean. For some strange reason, the bathroom floor was two feet higher than the bedroom floor with no step between! Watch that first step! We had a flushing toilet and a shower with running water but... no hot water! We quickly learned that the best time to take a shower was during our rest time in the afternoons when we were hot from being outside.

One night, my roommate Hope screamed as she saw a tiny mouse scurry across the floor. The busboy brought us a sheet of sticky paper to place under the bed. The next morning, I carried the paper and our uninvited guest down to the trash. The following morning I awoke earlier than Hope and quickly removed another sheet of sticky paper with two more unwanted house guests before she saw them. After that we were freed of additional guests… that is, until the last morning when the sticky paper had captured a two-inch hairy spider. He was under *my* bed. I am so glad that I didn't find him until the last morning or I would not have been able to sleep nights.

Sunday morning the local pastors came to the missions base to meet our team and to escort each of us to a different church to be their speaker for the day. We drove through some of the most beautiful countryside for almost an hour before arriving at the village church where I had the privilege of speaking that morning.

The people were so warm and loving; I felt very much at home in this quaint little concrete block church surrounded by so many beautiful jungle plants. After a lunch of chicken and white rice, we made our way back to our motel room for another quick rest period before heading out to another village and evening of ministry. We began by going door to door handing out flyers to invite them to come to the concert and open air service. About five o'clock, the concert began and the crowd began to fill the barangay (village) meeting place. No matter how poor the barangay, everyone we visited had a large meeting area with concrete floors and a metal roof with open sides, and quite often a stage and even bleachers. Although there were no walls, these structures offered shelter from the sun and rain and were perfect for our meetings.

After the invitation to receive Jesus as Lord of their life, we gave an invitation to come for prayer for daily needs and healings. Each of our team members had the privilege of praying for twenty to thirty people.

Monday through Friday, as soon as breakfast was finished, we headed off to the schools to tell the students about Jesus. What joy filled our hearts as entire classrooms prayed a prayer to invite Jesus into their lives. We gifted each student with a Bible study book and invited them to bring their family to the evening meeting in their village.

The days were packed to the maximum with visiting each class-room in five schools during the morning hours, door to door handing out flyers in the afternoons, and open-air services in the evenings. Also in the afternoons, part of our team would visit the village from the night before and meet with those who received

Christ to give them a Bible and establish them in a Bible study group.

One afternoon we were given free time to visit the local mall. It was amazing. We drove past blocks of makeshift stores, then all of a sudden there was this fabulous two-story modern mall that covered two city blocks in each direction. It was so unexpected.

We ate most of our meals at the mission base where local women prepared us boiled meat, mango, pineapple and white rice. We had rice for breakfast as a side dish to our eggs then more rice for lunch and dinner followed by sweetened white rice cake for dessert. When we visited a local restaurant, we were served a delicious barbecued chicken quarter and a generous portion of rice. As we ate, one of their employees came by and offered seconds of, you guessed it, white rice. We were then treated to a delightful dessert called "Hallo Hallo." Hallo Hallo is a dish of finely shaved ice topped with a scoop of ice cream and multiple berries. It is as colorful as it is delicious.

What an incredible opportunity to serve the Lord and see a part of the world I might never have seen. The Filipino people remain close to my heart.

From Cayuan, we went in a different direction each day to carry the gospel to all the surrounding villages. We traveled anywhere from thirty minutes to an hour, which allowed us to see a lot of the country while in route to minister. Cayuan is a city with a modern mall and traffic hustling and bustling day and night. The streets are crowded with motor scooters sprinting about dodging in and out as they make their way to their destination. There are no streetlights or stop signs. Drivers just politely wait as other drivers turn in front of them. It is hard to believe that just thirty minutes away from this busy, noisy city people still live in huts.

A NEW DIRECTION: COLOMBIA

From the pulpit of our church came an open invitation for anyone who wanted to be a part of the Colombia mission trip in June 2019. I began to pray and ask God if I should be a part of the team that summer. As I prayed, Heaven was silent. I attended the meeting and finally as the meeting was closing, I heard God say: "Go, and I will send you."

We sent out letters to the church family and to our friends and relatives asking for financial support. My support came in so rapidly —that is, all but $10. I thought $10 was no big deal, I will just drop that in myself. Then I heard God say: "No, I said, I will send you."

Sunday after church a little grandmother who was about 90 years old came running after me, pushing her walker as fast as she could go. "Donna, Donna," she called. "I've been looking for you. I want to give you some support money for your mission trip." She handed me... $10! Just then I chuckled in my heart as I recalled God saying, "Go, I will send you."

When we arrived in Colombia, I was delighted to see a modern motel complete with a swimming pool! My past two mission trips had very rustic accommodations. The rooms in this motel were modest with plain white walls and no closet but a modern toilet and shower (still no hot water, though). We were kept busy ministering all day long in the hot, humid Colombian weather, so a quick dip in the pool was pure delight before dragging off to bed.

Our purpose for going to Colombia was for each team member to partner with a small group of local parishioners to train them to evangelize their city. After the training session at the local church, we would then go house to house and help them practice their new skills.

One night, as we were in our motel, it began to rain. The rain came down in torrents. The next morning we began our day with a drive to a neighboring church to do an outreach there. The sun was shining and the paved highway was clear, allowing our vehicles to move speedily toward our destination. That is, until we arrived at our turn off and a dirt road. The storm from the night before had turned this next seven miles into quite a challenge, even for our four-wheel drive vehicles. We only went a short way before the vehicles began to slide in thick mud. At one point, my vehicle slid completely side ways on the road. We were going to have to walk. As we began our trek, a motorcycle with a cart attached came along and gave several of us a lift. We laughed loudly as we were jostled to and fro as our driver forced his little but mighty cycle through the mud. He had special equipment allowing his vehicle to manage the mud where the car had gotten stuck.

A wee bit later, more of our team arrived at the church riding in the back of a cattle truck. Finally, the team was all together again, feet and ankles muddy but in good spirits. After a bowl of chicken soup, we began our house to house evangelism through this beautiful jungle landscape.

All too soon, our week in Colombia was near its end. We had worked hard all week so as a treat, the last day there, the local pastor took us for a day at the beach. The sands of the beach were immaculate and the water was so clear you could see the bottom. Interestingly though, there were no waves at this beach.

As we enjoyed our fried fish lunch, a couple of native ladies came by and asked if they could give anyone a full massage for only about $10 for an hour. As several teammates received their massage, we in turn ministered the gospel message to the ladies. Both ladies received Jesus as their Lord and Savior. Our leader then asked if they would like to be baptized. What a glorious day.

The next morning we were to have breakfast in the motel dining room just before heading to the airport. As we prayed, one by one the Holy Spirit drew the motel staff to enter the room and ask for prayer. We had witnessed to them all week and now they, too, were hungry for God. We prayed with them and saw their countenance change to pure joy as they experienced God as their Savior and healer of their bodies.

We also taught them to pray for *each other*, something that hadn't crossed their minds. We stood back as they laid hands on each other and asked God for healing, restoration, and peace for one another—

and their prayers were answered! It was incredible to experience their joy and surprise at how God not only healed them, but used them to heal their co-workers.

It was evidence to us, as well, that God uses us wherever we are—whether it's the official assignment in the neighborhoods, or among the staff who served us meals, cleaned our clothes, and took care of our rooms.

It was an incredible week, one that will never be forgotten by any of us. We saw God move in powerful ways. What a joy to be invited to partner in His work with people He loves.

AFTERWORD

I am thankful that all four of my children and my stepdaughter are actively serving God. Cheri has become a licensed minister with a beautiful ministry to women. She is happily married to David, a mighty man of God who is a talented drummer in high demand for concerts. She has given me three wonderful grandsons. One of her boys, Christopher, was the first grandchild to be married in January, 2019. He has since given me my first great-grandchild, Gabriella.

Michele is totally in love with God and conducts the Bible study in-home group I hostess each week. It is a blessing that God allows me to use my home for this ministry. I love being able to be part of her group as she so ably shares Jesus with her peers. Michele is a courtroom reporter and God has already opened the doors for her to record city council minutes. She is mom to two loving college-aged boys. Her oldest son, Kenny, is a chef in a high-class restaurant and his younger brother, Michael, is a waiter. God has blessed her with a new husband, Curtis.

Debbie and her husband Mark co-teach the two- and three-year-old Sunday school class in their church. They have a good marriage and three handsome sons. Their oldest boy, Jonathan, is a gifted artist and is in his first year of college. Matthew attends high school and

Jacob is in junior high. Debbie ministers to her 76-year-old dad, Wesley, by driving him each week to purchase groceries.

Billy also teaches a weekly Bible study and is taking classes to become a computer programmer. He is yet to be married which makes it possible for him to share my home with me, a huge blessing. Although he works swing shift and is gone five nights a week, he is still here often enough to be a companion and a prayer partner.

My stepdaughter Jessica is also a wonderful woman of God. She has gone to Africa for the last two summers on missions trips and is planning yet another trip there this summer. She has given me a precious granddaughter, Alexandria, who is a gorgeous blue-eyed blonde eight-year-old. Jessica and her daughter live five hours away across the Sierra Nevada mountains. Consequently, we can't visit as frequently as we would like, but I treasure those times when we are able to enjoy time together. She is a very loving daughter.

After renting out the family home for three years, during which time Billy and I shared an apartment, I decided to sell the house and purchase a new, smaller home. God blessed me with a newly remodeled 1400 square-foot home with three bedrooms and two bathrooms. The kitchen has fifteen feet of counter space and, with the open floor plan, is ideal for hosting Bible studies and other groups. It is perfectly located just one mile from my two youngest girls and a mere 45 minutes to Cheri and David's home.

The restorers of the home did the entire insides but left the yard untouched. When Billy and I moved in, the back fence was a disaster. The previous owner had used anything he could get to mend that fence. I decided that the fence would be my first project. As I prayed about who to hire, I felt God urge me to go outside and look behind it. To my surprise, behind the ugly fence was a perfectly good fence! All Billy and I needed to do was remove the makeshift fence. The neighbor behind us had built a fence so they didn't have to look at the ugly one. Gardening is my hobby so having a non-planted yard has been a delight for me to tackle. Now the yard is as lovely as the interior.

At Michael's funeral four people accepted Christ. That made all we went through worth it.

I donated Michael's truck to the church and the bread ministry has continued, led by some of the men in the church. We had also started a Bible study at the motel where we delivered bread and Wesley has continued that ministry. It blesses me to see these others continue on in the work of God.

As a 70-year-old widow, I feel especially blessed to have all four of my children and their families within forty-five minutes of my home and to enjoy their love for me as well as a mutual love for our God. I can't wait to see the rest of God's plan for my life as we make this journey together with my hand in His.

God has been my source of strength, my shield in storms, my great provider and my protector when the enemy would have killed me. I do not know what the future holds but I know Who holds my future and that I am indeed His.

Remember that empty calendar I was so worried about when I first retired? It's not empty now! After returning from Colombia on my third mission trip, my son and I enrolled in a discipleship class at church that meets three nights a week—Mondays, Wednesdays, and Saturdays.

During the days, Billy and I co-host a Bible study on Wednesday mornings, I hostess a sewing party every Thursday to continue making dresses for the Christmas shoeboxes, and on Fridays, Billy and I have resumed going out to the homeless. Empty calendar? Nope! Give your days to God and He will give you the fullest life yet! AND the discipleship class we are enrolled in is talking about a mission trip at the end of this year, 2021.

God has taken all of the broken pieces of my life and restored me.

Loved and Protected!

ABOUT THE AUTHOR

Pastors' daughter, Bible teacher, and pastor's wife, Donna began teaching God's word when she was a young teen. Now retired, she has enjoyed missionary ventures to Haiti, Philippines, and Colombia. Her three adult daughters and son are each currently teaching the Bible, thus continuing the family heritage.

Made in the USA
Columbia, SC
16 September 2021